Greenhill Books

U-Boat
War Patrol

U-Boat War Patrol

THE HIDDEN PHOTOGRAPHIC DIARY OF *U 564*

Lawrence Paterson

GREENHILL BOOKS, LONDON
STACKPOLE BOOKS, PENNSYLVANIA

Greenhill Books

U-Boat War Patrol
First published 2004 by
Greenhill Books, Lionel Leventhal Limited,
Park House, 1 Russell Gardens, London NW11 9NN
and
Stackpole Books, 5067 Ritter Road, Mechanicsburg,
PA 17055, USA

British Library Cataloguing in Publication Data:
Paterson, Lawrence
U-boat war patrol: the hidden photographic diary of U-564
1. Suhren, Teddy
2. Germany, Kriegsmarine – History
3. World War, 1939–1945 – Naval operations – Submarine
4. World War, 1939–1945 – Naval operations, German
2.   I. Title
3.   940.5'451

1-85367-575-X

Library of Congress Cataloging-in-Publication Data available

Edited, designed and typeset by Roger Chesneau
Printed and bound in Thailand

To Audrey 'Mumbles' Paterson

≡ Contents

All times quoted in this book are in German Summer Time (the standard time kept aboard U-boats) unless otherwise noted.

Preface

FIFTY-FIVE years after the end of the Second World War in Europe, history's long arm reached out from the distant shadows of long silent battlefields to the most unlikely of places. During April 2000, in a tiny Post Office at Staintondale, on the edge of the Yorkshire Moors, a unique time capsule arrived unexpectedly into the hands of the Post Office's owner Frank James. Twenty black-and-white photographs, some dappled with age, were handed over by a man unsure of their provenance, or indeed of what to do with them. The photographs showed young men aboard a submarine, the national cockade on their caps surmounted by an eagle clutching in its talons the unmistakable swastika symbol of the Third Reich. Obviously it was a U-boat crew, but who they were, and where, remained a mystery to Frank.

With an interest in all aspects of history, but no knowledge of the U-Boat Service, Frank proceeded to research what he could about the random photographs. Aiding him enormously was the fact that most boats carried an unofficial symbol, a distinctive *Wappen* (emblem, or coat of arms) painted somewhere on the conning tower. In this case it was instantly recognisable—a large black cat, tail held proudly upright and back arched over the digits '3X'. Although some fourteen U-boats carried cats as part of their *Wappen*, this must be one of the five U-boats that carried the *dreimal schwarze Kater* symbol— 'Three Black Cats'. In turn it soon became apparent that the photographs were all taken aboard *U 564*, commanded by the legendary Reinhard 'Teddy' Suhren.

Foster Appleyard, a wartime Royal Navy diver and postwar landlord of a small public house in Bradford, had given Frank's visitor the photographs. Although Appleyard had since died, there was more of the collection to be found in the safekeeping of a friend of the deceased diver. On the proviso that they be properly archived and researched, a shoebox full of photographs arrived in Staintondale soon afterwards, bringing the grand total to 361.

It transpired that Appleyard had been part of the extensive team of naval personnel involved during 1944 and 1945 in clearing the massive amount of debris and detritus of battle from the French harbour at Brest, in Brittany. Brest had been one of five French ports taken over in 1940 by the conquering German *Wehrmacht* with the express purpose of converting them to forward U-boat bases. Stationed in Brest, *U 564* had been part of the 1st U-Boat Flotilla, a unit whose Type VIIC boats ranged as far west as the Caribbean Sea in the grim battle of attrition against Allied convoy traffic that stretched between the New World and the Old across the expansive wastes of the North Atlantic.

As the tide of war swung inexorably against the Germans, the beleaguered U-boat service was pushed back until its submarines were fighting running battles against a superior enemy off the coast of France itself. In August 1944 Brest was finally besieged by American soldiers of General Patton's Third Army, racing from the Normandy beaches towards Brittany. A month of savage and costly street fighting against German paratroopers, infantry and naval personnel ended with the city's eventual surrender to the Allies, who then faced the arduous task of evaluating the harbour for possible use as a supply head for advancing Allied forces in France. It soon became apparent that the harbour was useless: not only was it clogged with scuttled and destroyed shipping, but the capture of the deep-water port of Cherbourg and the unexpectedly rapid advance of the Allies towards Germany rendered Brest too far from the front lines and surplus to requirements.

During his work in Brest's shattered remains, Appleyard had followed the majority of troops stationed there and explored the cavernous interior of the port's imposing concrete U-boat pens. Within the labyrinthine interior, Appleyard stumbled across the collection of photographs, 'liberating' them and eventually returning to Yorkshire with them in his haversack. Thus, nearly sixty years later, the collection again saw the light of day and was soon on its way to a photographic archive in Gosport, England.

Frank had taken his research as far as he could, and, after enquiries to several U-boat-related museums and archives had yielded nothing, he approached Debbie Corner, Keeper of Photographs at the Royal Navy Submarine Museum in Gosport, home of the Second World War British submarine fleet. Debbie instantly recognised the importance of the photographs, and they were soon housed securely within the Museum's collection in pristine blue folders, where they remain still. Despite, obviously, focusing on the Royal Navy's own submarine service, the Museum holds a great many U-boat photographs and related records, often overlooked by researchers and writers.

At this point I entered the story. After several years living in France, near Brest, researching the *Kriegsmarine* and its U-boat service, my wife and I returned to England as I was putting the finishing touches to a book on the history of the 1st U-Boat Flotilla. I soon became involved with the Archive Working Group within the Submarine Museum, my particular role being to assist with all U-boat related material. After organising and beginning to catalogue the huge numbers of U-boat photographs, I turned once again to the 'Appleyard Collection', and the exceptional study of Suhren's U-boat patrol during the summer of 1942. Many gaps remained in piecing together the story that unfolded with each photograph, and soon it became a full-time research operation in Germany, England and France. This book is the result.

An entire collection that charts the course of a single patrol is a rare find indeed, and *U 564*'s successes and trials provide a unique insight into life aboard the medium-size U-boats. Taken during the summer of 1942 by an onboard war correspondent, the photographs show a U-boat in action within the Atlantic and Caribbean, as the German submarine service teetered on the brink of what was, with hindsight, the unstoppable downward slide into defeat. However, at the stage of the war at which they were taken, U-boats could still spend time surfaced without fear of Allied air attack within the mid-Atlantic and were raking a harvest of considerable numbers of Allied merchant ships.

The German crew are shown in virtually every station, and several other U-boats and their commanders also feature within the photographs as the 'wolfpacks' gathered to fight or be resupplied. Most of these pictures are previously unpublished; many of the photos are taken from segments of newsreel shown as part of the weekly cinema record of the war for German theatre audiences; and a select few were taken by Joseph Goebbels' Propaganda Ministry for inclusion in the magazines *Signal* and *Die Kriegsmarine*. Accompanying the reproductions of those photographs now housed in Gosport are a few selected from the files of the *U-Boot Archiv* in Altenbruch, Germany. There, too, are many photographs taken aboard *U 564* or involving the crew at leisure in Brest, most of them having been 'snapped' unofficially. The reason for the breadth of material relating to *U 564* can perhaps be explained by the character of her commander, Reinhard 'Teddy' Suhren.

Teddy remains legendary within the U-boat world. Fondly remembered for his good nature and command ability as much for his irreverent and rebellious wit that frequently led to brushes with authority, Suhren was a dynamic member of the German Navy. One of the most highly decorated men of the élite German submarine service, Suhren fired more successful torpedo shots than any other man during the war, most while still a watch officer aboard *U 48* prior to taking his own command. However, it is not his remarkable combat record that causes a now-familiar sparkle to enter the eye of every U-boat veteran that I speak to, nearly sixty years after the end of the war; rather, it was Teddy's perpetual reluctance to conform to the rigidity of thought desired by National Socialist Germany. Veterans spend time recounting numerous tales of Teddy's tribulations with those in authority above him. However, despite this trait, Suhren found himself at times remarkably close to the centre of power within Germany, earning the second highest *Wehrmacht* award for valour, being invited to stay with Martin Bormann and his family, and even dancing with Eva Braun. He was ultimately one of the lucky third of all U-boat men to survive the dreadful casualty rate during the war. He died of stomach cancer in 1984.

It had long been my desire to write a biography of this unique man and his wartime career, but he had already put so much of it down in his inimitable style within an autobiography named *Nasses Eichenlaub* (Wet Oak Leaves), edited by Fritz Brustat-Naval in 1984. Gesa Suhren vividly remembers her father dictating the story to his wife Hannelore, who painstakingly typed the entire manuscript. Thus, this book seeks to illustrate life onboard *U 564* at the period when the outcome of the U-boat war hung in the balance. However, Suhren's widow Hannelore and daughter Gesa have also related a multitude of anecdotes of Teddy's exploits, and no study of *U 564* could begin without a look at this extraordinary man's career up to 1942, when *U 564* put to sea from Brest carrying a war correspondent to record her journey into Atlantic action.

L. P.

≡ Acknowledgements

AS ALWAYS, the writing of a book like this would be impossible without help and support from a great number of people. First of all I would like to thank Sarah Paterson for her help with archive research and travelling the length and breadth of Germany in search of clues, and Audrey, Shane, Ray, Megan and James Paterson for their constant support and encouragement. Secondly, enormous thanks are due to Frank James, without whom this collection would not have come to light, and who did an extraordinary amount of research on its provenance.

Of course, the photographic compilation would not have featured at all without the kind permission and help of Debbie Corner, the Keeper of Photographs at Gosport's Royal Navy Submarine Museum. Maggie Bidmead, the Keeper of Archives at the RNSM also helped with information, encouragement and fine afternoon chats in her office — as well as, later, proof-reading the whole book for me.

The preparation of this manuscript was aided enormously by Elizabeth Burbridge, who allowed me to occupy what once was her library and is now my cluttered office! More impeccable proof-reading by Tonya Allen has helped me to avoid the many mistakes that my less-than-perfect typing creates, and her wide knowledge of the subject matter helped me to check my facts. Lionel Leventhal and the entire staff of Greenhill Books have made the production of this work a pleasure.

For information, help or inspiration I am deeply indebted to the following people: Frau Hannelore Suhren, Gesa Suhren, Erik Lawaetz, Frau Lawaetz, Hans Hausruckinger, Jak Mallmann-Showell, Ted Savas, Carlo Guzzi, Ralf Bublitz, Jürgen Weber and the *München U-Boot-Kameradschaft*, Mats Karlsson, Siri Lawson, Deborah Eaton (Head Librarian and Keeper of the Emden Naval Collection, St Edmund Hall, Oxford), Jurgen Schlemm (Editor of the excellent *Das Archiv*), Frans Beckers, Ulrich and Cristel Zimmermann, Erhard Holthusen and the Deutches Haus 'Rowdy Table', Peter Carlow (the 'B. C. of U-Boats'), David Beasley (godfather of the Portsmouth car parking scheme), 'Saint' Mike and his never-ending supply of paper, Bruce

Dickinson, Dave Murray, Adrian Smith, Steve Harris, Clive Burr, Nicko McBrain, the courteous and helpful staff of Kew's Public Records Office, and Horst and Annmarie Bredow of Altenbruch's *U-Boot Archiv*.

My most sincere thanks go to the many veterans of this terrible conflict who have shared their knowledge and memories with me. In particular, I would like to mention Herbert Waldschmidt (*U 564, U 146, U 2374* and *U 4719*), Herman Hausruckinger (*U 564*), Jürgen Oesten (*U 61, U 106* and *U 861*), Georg Seitz (*U 604* and *U 873*), Hans Rudolf Rösing (*U 48*), Ludwig Stoll (*U 148*), Horst Bredow (*U 288*) and Claus Peter Carlsen (*U 732*).

L. P.

Glossary, Abbreviations

A	(German) *Achtzig Meter*, KTB shorthand meaning 'eighty metres'. Thus a boat at a depth of 110 metres could be referred to as 'A+30'.
ASDIC	Term applied to the sonar equipment used for locating submerged submarines. A powerful and effective weapon, it emitted a distinct 'ping' when locating the target. The word is an acronym for Anti-Submarine Detection Committee, the organisation that began research into this device in 1917.
BdU	(German) *Befehlshaber der Unterseeboote,* or Commander U-Boats.
'Bold'	(German) Short for *Kobold* (goblin), an acoustic decoy, known also as the 'submarine bubble target', comprising a small, cylindrical, mesh container filled with calcium hydride. When ejected from a submerged U-boat, the compound reacted with sea water and gave off hydrogen bubbles—and thus a false echo to ASDIC operators. It was simple but effective.
cbm	Cubic metres
'Eel'	(German) *Aal*, a slang expression for torpedo.
'Enigma'	(German) Coding machine used by German Armed Forces throughout the Second World War.
FdU	(German) *Führer der Unterseeboote*, or Flag Officer for Submarines, responsible for a particular geographical region.
grt	Gross registered tonnage (or tons). A standard measurement of the size of a merchant ship, one ton equalling 100 cubic feet of cargo capacity.
Ing.	(German) *Ingenieur*, or engineering grade, e.g. *Kaptlt (Ing)*.
Kriegsmarine	(German) Navy of the Third Reich.
KTB	(German) *Kriegstagebuch*, or War Diary. Kept by the commander during a U-boat's patrol. His handwritten version was later typed for the official records. It included torpedo firing diagrams.
LI	(German) *Leitender Ingenieur*, or Chief Engineer.
'Lords'	(German) Slang term for naval ratings.
Luftwaffe	(German) Air Force.
OKM	(German) *Oberkommando der Kriegsmarine*, or Navy High Command.
OKW	(German) *Oberkommando der Wehrmacht*, or Armed Forces High Command.
Ritterkreuz	(German) Knight's Cross of the Iron Cross.

Sperrbrecher	(German) Barrage -breaker — a specialized mine destructor vessel.
Turm	(German) Conning tower.
U-Bootwaffe	(German) U-Boat Service.
UZO	(German) *Überwasserzieloptik*, or surface targeting device.
VLR	(British) Very Long Range. Used in conjunction with aircraft, often Liberators.
Vorpostenboot	(German) Coastal patrol boat (or ship).
Wabo	(German) *Wasserbombe(n)*, or depth charge(s).
Wachoffizier	(German) Watch Officer. There were three separate U-boat watch crews, each consisting of an officer, a petty officer and two ratings. The ship's First Watch Officer (IWO) would be the Executive Officer (second-in-command), the Second Watch Officer (IIWO) the ship's designated Second Officer, and the Third Watch Officer (IIIWO) often the *Obersteuermann* (Navigation Officer). Their duties were typically divided into the following time frames: 0000 – 0400 (1st Watch), 0400–0800 (2nd Watch) and 0800–1200 (3rd Watch); and then 1200–1600 (1st Watch), 1600–2000 (2nd Watch) and 2000–2400 (3rd Watch). The duties of the IWO included the care and maintenance of the torpedo and firing system as well as the control of surface attacks; the IIWO handled administration regarding food and supplies as well as the operation of deck and flak weapons.
Wehrmacht	(German) Armed Forces.
'Wintergarten'	(German) Nickname given to the open-railed extension astern of the conning tower, built to accommodate increased flak weaponry and known to the Allies as a 'bandstand'.

Table of Ranks

German	British/American
Grossadmiral	Admiral of the Fleet/Fleet Admiral
Admiral	Admiral
Vizeadmiral (VA)	Vice-Admiral
Konteradmiral (KA)	Rear-Admiral
Kapitän zur See (KzS)	Captain
Fregattenkapitän (FK)	Commander
Korvettenkapitän (KK)	Commander
Kapitänleutnant (Kptlt)	Lieutenant-Commander
Oberleutnant zur See (ObltzS)	Lieutenant
Leutnant zur See (LzS)	Sub Lieutenant/Lieutenant (j.g.)
Fähnrich	Midshipman
Stabsobersteuermann	Senior Quartermaster/Warrant Quartermaster
Obermaschinist	Senior Machinist/Warrant Machinist
Bootsmann	Boatswain
Oberbootsmannsmaat	Boatswain's Mate Second Class
Bootsmannsmaat	Coxswain
Mechanikermaat	Torpedo Petty Officer
-maat (trade inserted at dash)	Petty Officer
Maschinenobergefreiter	Leading Seaman Machinist
Funkobergefreiter	Leading Seaman Telegraphist
Matrosenobergefreiter	Leading Seaman
Maschinengefreiter	Able Seaman Machinist
Matrosengefreiter	Able Seaman

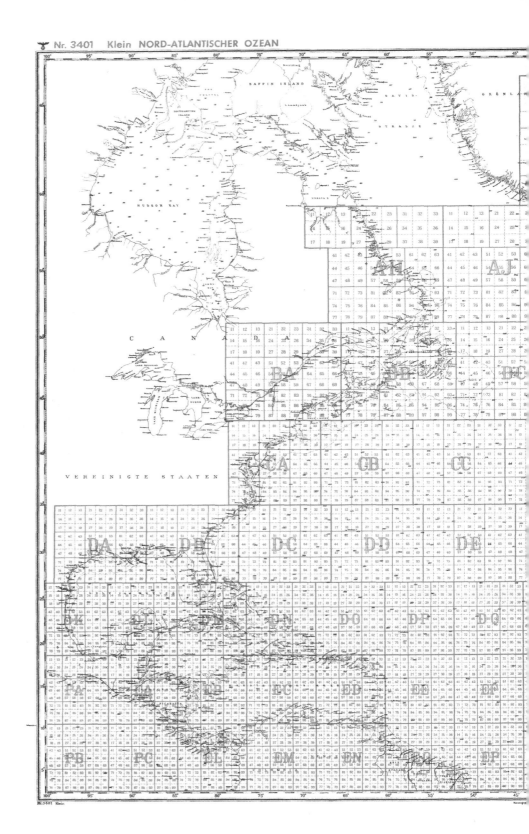

Nur für den Dienstgebrauch!

Dies ist ein geheimer Gegenstand. Mißbrauch ist strafbar.

Für die Navigierung nicht zu benutzen

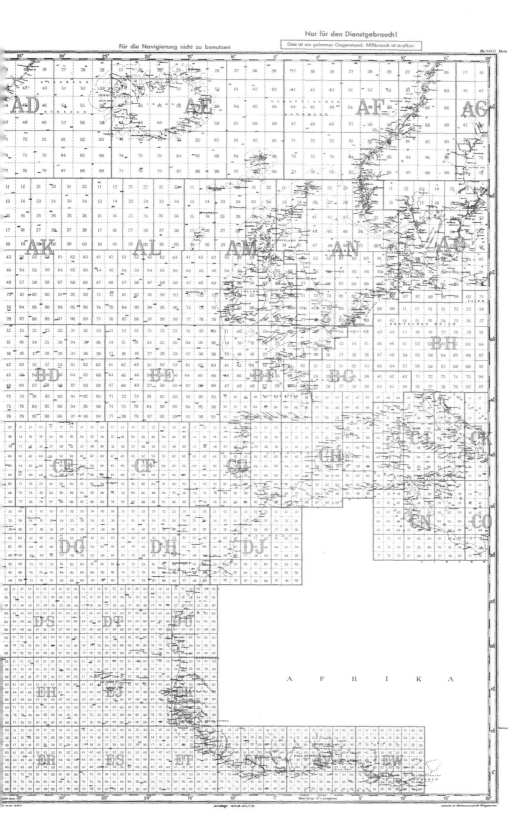

☰ Introduction

REINHARD 'Teddy' Suhren entered the U-boat service in 1938, already carrying a reputation for outspokenness and honesty that did not always sit easily with superior officers. Possessed of a passion for life that manifested itself in a raucous sense of humour, Teddy soon felt at home within Dönitz's élite corps where the maverick often reigned supreme: 'They [the Flotilla] all liked him. He was widely known; he was an original. There was but one Teddy Suhren.'[1]

Suhren had already led a tumultuous career since enlisting in the German Navy at the age of eighteen, and it was a trend that continued through the years that followed. He was born Reinhard Johann Heinz Paul Anton Suhren on 16 April 1916 at his grandmother's house in Langenschwalbach, west of Frankfurt. His parents, Geert and Ernestine Ludovika, had only recently returned to the Fatherland after their expulsion from Samoa, an Imperial German colony annexed by New Zealand troops at the outbreak of war.

At the dawn of the twentieth century, the newborn country of Germany had cast around for territories—leftovers from the more mature European powers' empire building. Germany soon established dominion over several African and Pacific states, among them Samoa. Anxious to expand the farming and trade potential of her new protectorate, she encouraged settlers to emigrate to the lush Samoan islands, and among them was Geert Suhren, a recent graduate of Halle's agricultural courses. In 1913 he returned to Germany from Apia, where he had made his home and established a thriving plantation named Tafaigata. His stay in Europe was brief—long

An uncharacteristically bearded Teddy Suhren returns from successful patrol to the coast of the United States, June 1942. Around his neck he wears the red scarf knitted by his mother – a talisman he rarely removed while at sea.

enough to marry Ernestine Ludovika—before returning to Samoa. A year later, on 16 May 1914, a son was born in Apia to the contented pair, named Gerd as family tradition demanded for any first-born male.

Their paradise was to be short-lived. In June 1914 the Austrian Archduke Franz Ferdinand was assassinated in Sarajevo, and within weeks Europe was at war. New Zealand soldiers rapidly arrived to claim German Samoa as a New Zealand protectorate, and the South Seas idyll was over for the Suhren family. Geert, Ernestine and their infant son travelled from Pago-Pago to San Francisco and on to Europe under the assumed name of 'Mr and Mrs Gasket' aboard a Norwegian steamship. Geert had managed to mask his pronounced duelling scars—a sure mark of German University education—beneath a heavy beard, promptly shaved off after arrival in Germany and his enlistment into the *Ulanen*, the 18th Leipzig Lancers. Leaving his wife and son with Ernestine's mother in Langenschwalbach, *Oberleutnant* Suhren was sent to the Russian Front, where he soon acquitted himself well, earning the Iron Cross for valour. By the end of 1916 he had also been awarded the *Ritterkreuz der Militär-Sankt-Heinrichs-Orden* (Knight's Cross of the Military Order of St Heinrich), Saxony's second highest decoration for conspicuous personal bravery on the battlefield during the fierce fighting against Russian troops of General Alexei Brusilov's southern offensive.[2] His regimental report read: 'By means of his personal bravery and iron strength of will, he took charge of the *Ulanen*, who were exhausted by previous strenuous fighting and days of marching, and after a twelve-hour battle took control of Tuliczew in the face of strongly consolidated Russian positions.'

In November 1918 Germany requested, and was granted, an armistice, but this was followed by many years of internal strife and unrest. The country's manpower and resources had been bled dry both by four years of unrelenting war and by the harsh surrender terms of the Versailles Treaty. The Suhrens were among those to suffer from runaway inflation, and they, among nameless other millions, were soon stricken by poverty. There was no question of a return to Samoa to reclaim their lost plantation, but, using his agricultural training to the utmost, Geert Suhren became Director of Agricultural Production for Saxony.

Even at that stage of their lives, the characters of the two young Suhren brothers were clearly defined. Gerd and Reinhard were almost two sides of the same coin: 'I daresay in a way they were similar, but in other ways they were very different. . . . Gerd was far more introspective, quieter than Teddy was. . . . He was perhaps a more noble edition of the Suhren brotherhood, more refined.'[3] A third sibling soon joined the inseparable brothers, a sister named Almut, whose disposition more closely resembled that of her eldest brother. While Gerd was studious and quiet, intensely interested in engineering with his keenly analytical mind, Reinhard was boisterous and high-spirited, his perpetual grin the bane of many teachers and figures of authority. It was a personality trait that would survive with him through the difficult years that followed.

Reinhard went through a succession of schools; hw was, in his own words, 'not particularly industrious, but I survived.' Along the way, he developed a love of horseriding and sailing. This latter skill was particularly encouraged by time at the Hermann Lietz School in Spiekeroog, a rural boarding school modelled along English lines. As soon as they were old enough, the two brothers learnt to drive and ride motorcycles, displaying the kind of calm under pressure that would later become a hallmark of their military service: 'Their confidence on the road was most unusual, as was their unerring ability to make important decisions in moments of danger.'[4]

Later, in their mid-teens, Reinhard and Gerd attended the state secondary Deutsche Oberschule at Bautzen, riding by motorcycle from their home at Drehsa. During the final summer of his education, Reinhard applied to attend a sailing course in Neustadt, hoping to sharpen his skills. In the newly militarised Germany, an emphasis was placed on parade-ground manoeuvres in even so innocuous an

Suhren (left) as a *Fähnrich* during his turbulent cadetship.

activity as sailing tuition, and, having applied to join the Navy after graduation, Reinhard was determined to impress. Soon his five-foot four-inch tall figure was joining the other students in learning to march. It was here that he acquired his nickname. During the parade drill of the young students, the adolescent cadet in the following rank suddenly began to laugh: 'My goodness, Reinhard, your marching makes you look like a teddy bear!'[5] Unimpressed with the inferred derision at his less than military appearance, Suhren chose to ignore the remark and concentrated on keeping his left foot separated from his right.

It was in Bautzen that Reinhard finally took his school leaving exams (*Abitur*) in 1935 and prepared to begin further training for his adult career. He had felt himself drawn initially towards medicine, a vocation that ran in his mother's ancestry. His great-grandfather had been consultant gynæcologist to the Grand-Duchess of Hessen-Nassau, Queen Victoria's daughter. From there he had also attended the *Tsarina* in Russia, Princess Alice von Hessen, who had inherited the haemophilia that blighted Victoria's bloodline. But Reinhard was also attracted to the sea, and it was perhaps his brother Gerd entering the *Reichsmarine* as a cadet-engineering officer during 1933 that made his mind up for him. On 5 April 1935 he enlisted as a trainee line officer, attached to the 2nd Naval Division within what was now known as the *Kriegsmarine*: 'My father, an old hand at these things, gave me a piece of advice for the road: You can't do anything, you don't know anything; to start with make yourself out to be a dimwit — and be grateful that you are in a position to learn so many new things that are important for your life. And that advice has never yet been proved wrong.'[6]

By 1935 Adolf Hitler's National Socialist Workers' Party was enjoying its third year of power. New prosperity was revitalising Germany, and the armed forces were among those institutions that benefited. However, there were many who feared an ill future with their new government. In the Suhren household, Geert was one of those conservatives that doubted the intentions and abilities of the Nazi regime. This attitude rubbed off on Reinhard, who had always listened to his father's wisdom. However, in April 1935, at the age of eighteen, the subject of politics was far from Reinhard's mind as he travelled to Dänholm to begin his basic naval training as part of *2 Kompanie/II Schiffsstammabteilung der Ostsee*. There the new draft of officer cadets started three months of infantry-style physical training, Reinhard's squad under the command of the East Prussian *Bootsmaat* Jodeit. Although he remembered him fondly in his autobiography,

Reinhard, with his unfaltering ability to see the humour in any situation, coupled with an insolent grin and innocent gaze, became the target for a great deal of Jodeit's disapproval, much to the amusement of the rest of the squad:

> '*Matrose* Suhren, do you know what you are?'
> 'No Herr *Bootsmaat*'
> 'You are an ape. What are you?'
> 'I am an ape, *Herr Bootsmaat*.'
> '*Matrose* Suhren . . . these boots of yours are a disgrace to the entire German Navy.'
> 'Yes, *Herr Bootsmaat*.'
> 'What do you mean "Yes"? Are you trying to give me shit . . . ?'[7]

The hapless *Matrose* Reinhard Suhren marched and double-marched around Dänholm in his 'diceboxes', too large for his small feet. His slight figure soon became a familiar sight hopping around the parade ground with rifle at arm's length or lugging machine guns over sand dunes as punishment. He also bumped into his old friend from Neustadt, now a member of a sister training division. Sighting Suhren, he bellowed a greeting across the parade ground, using his nickname 'Teddy' to attract Suhren's attention and prompting peals of laughter from his comrades. Much to his annoyance at the extremely 'unmasculine' nickname, it stuck with his fellow cadets and became his new name. Eventually, once his pride recovered from the dig at his stature, Teddy resigned himself to his fate and accepted the new sobriquet, soon using it himself in general preference to his 'thoroughly Germanic' real one.

Three months of basic training were followed by a further three months sail training aboard the square-rigger *Gorch Fock*, which criss-crossed the Baltic and North Sea. Teddy was frequently stationed at the top of the mainmast, the smallest man on board and the natural choice for such a lofty position. A brief accident while under anchor near Fehmarn earned him a badly bruised leg after being caught between the ship's cutter and hull in a rising sea; but it was not enough to delay Teddy's training, and after three months of physiotherapy he was back atop the mast.

From there, Teddy and the rest of 'Crew 35' became *Seekadetten* and transferred *en masse* to the cruiser *Emden* for a nine-month foreign cruise to the Azores, the Caribbean and through the Panama Canal into the Pacific.[8] As a prospective *Fähnrich zur See*, Teddy saw little of the foreign ports that he visited on board *Emden*. Run ragged by the ship's regular crew, the intake of midshipmen was put through their paces in their first taste of foreign service.

Finally, after their nine-month voyage, Teddy and his fellow 400 draftees were moved ashore to the famous 'Red Castle by the Sea' — the Marineschule (Naval Academy) at Mürwik, east of Flensburg. There the recruits would be schooled in all aspects of being a naval officer — navigation, signals, engineering, tactics, leadership, maritime law, mathematics and English — as well as the more genteel arts of dancing, fencing, riding and sailing. Teddy flourished. Excelling particularly at artillery school, he amassed high marks for his overall service aptitude, totalling 7.5 out of a possible 9. However, even while doing well, he invoked the ire of the academy's commander. Teddy's superb eyesight enabled him to gauge with extreme accuracy the fall of shot of his own artillery fire and make rapid readjustments so that he was able to score direct hits within three attempts, shortcutting the long-winded official method of fire adjustment by using his own judgement. Singled out for praise by the school's commandant, *Fähnrich* Suhren inadvertently allowed himself to speak too plainly and criticised the 'accepted method' of adjusting fire, earning for himself a dressing-down before the stifled laughter of his classmates. Nevertheless, even that could not prevent his excellent grading, and he continued to head his class — until *Rosenmontag*, 1936.

A Rhineland tradition, the Rose Monday Festival heralded a carnival in nearby Flensburg, and all midshipmen were granted leave until 6 a.m., apart from those within Teddy's division. His divisional commander had curtailed their free time to end at 5 a.m. — a fact that Teddy promptly forgot as the beer, wine and dancing continued into the early morning. Realising at the last moment that he, unlike his fellow-revellers, had to be back by 5 a.m., Teddy was mortified to arrive several minutes late for his curfew after a last-minute dash by taxi to the Marineschule. Inevitably, the guard officer reported him, and once again Teddy stood on the carpet before his furious superiors, his mere presence seeming to inflame their rage all the more. Most hurtful to the anxious Teddy was that his divisional officer, *Kapitänleutnant* Walther Kölle, who had awarded him such high marks during the previous weeks, stood silently and failed to defend him while Suhren was verbally torn apart. The consequences could have been disastrous. In a few short weeks, the draft was scheduled to take its Seaman Officer's exams, the service aptitude marks combining with examination results to give each cadet's final grade. Teddy's 7.5 was slashed to a 4 — equivalent to being reduced from a class leader to the bottom grade. He would never forgive what he took as a betrayal by Kölle, but one day, in the middle of the Atlantic, he would have some small measure of satisfaction.

Eventually he graduated, passing the exam with high marks and thereby enabling his aptitude score to be balanced, providing the required pass mark. But his record was permanently tarnished, and it followed him immediately to his first proper assignment as a *Fähnrich* aboard the destroyer *Max Schultz*, attached to Swinemünde's First Destroyer Division. There, the heavens seemed to rain misfortune on the hapless Teddy as the ship's Captain, Martin Baltzer, took an instant dislike to the young man: 'Apparently my mere appearance was tantamount to a provocation, especially since I was the smallest and didn't pussyfoot around and didn't allow myself to be brow-beaten. I was myself, and determined to stay so.'[9] As his close friend and fellow *Fähnrich* Jürgen Sander put it, in his thick Berlin accent,

> I tell you, once you've got yourself well and truly in the shit nothing can help you; you're always in the shit. However hard you try, even if you come out with top marks, no one notices any more, and at the end of the day the Old Man is determined to shit on you too for treading his corns too hard into the deck![10]

At one point Teddy even considered leaving the Navy, confiding his intention to his brother Gerd — by then a commissioned Engineering Officer — whose horrified response and help in influencing the opinion of those above him persuaded Teddy to stay. Finally, upon graduation as *Leutnant zur See* on 1 April 1938 Teddy volunteered and was transferred to the *U-Bootwaffe*, and a whole new world that welcomed, indeed valued, unconventional officers and independent thought opened before him. Teddy had at last found his place.

He was posted to the Watch Officer's Training Course, stationed aboard *U 1*, where he began to learn the tools of his new trade. The informal atmosphere and camaraderie peculiar to Dönitz's small corps appealed enormously to Teddy, and he thrived accordingly. As he settled into his new life, during November 1938 he was

assigned to the 'Wegener' Flotilla as an officer aboard *U 48*, then under construction in Kiel's Germaniawerft shipyard. 'Wegener' was the seventh U-boat flotilla within Dönitz's fledgeling service and at the time of Teddy's arrival boasted four boats (*U 45*, *U 46*, *U 47* and *U 51*), with a further four, including Teddy's, nearing completion. Standards were extremely high in the pre-war submarine force, and suitable officers were in short supply. To remedy the lack of trained men and also to grant a wider experience base for those who had graduated into its ranks, Dönitz rotated any 'spare' men through the available U-boats. Thus Teddy found himself as IIWO on three of the four 'Wegener' boats—*U 51*, *U 46* and *U 47*. The experience aboard each differed as widely as the individual commander's temperaments. While the calm and assured *Kaptlt* Ernst-Günter Heinicke (*U 51*) and *Kaptlt* Herbert Sohler (*U 46*) were veteran naval officers of a decade's experience, the mercurial *Kaptlt* Günther Prien (*U 47*) was one of the draft of merchant marine officers transferred into the *Kriegsmarine* after the loss of most of the officer's Crew 33 during the tragic sinking of the training ship *Niobe*. Tough, able and passionate about his trade, Prien had a harsh personality, able to whip any man found lacking to ribbons with his blistering wit. Teddy was not among those to earn Prien's disapproval, however, and he thrived. While aboard *U 47*, he absorbed the unorthodox nature of successful submarine command from one of Germany's legendary

A more familiar pose—but a far from natural one: Reinhard Suhren pictured at the Brest Naval Academy, headquarters of the First U-Boat Flotilla, after his award of the Oak Leaves to the Knight's Cross and his promotion to *Kapitänleutnant*.

fighting men, also forming a strong bond of friendship with the friendly, quiet—and equally short in stature—Engelbert 'Bertl' Endrass, Prien's IWO.

During 1938, the entire circle of U-boat officers within Dönitz's élite corps were known to each other. Flotilla loyalties elevated the bond so that those of the 'Wegener' flotilla remained the closest of friends into the difficult years that followed. Finally, on a spring morning in April 1939 Teddy and his crew stood before their commander as the *Kriegsmarine* ensign was raised for the first time and *U 48* prepared to begin service. Here Teddy brushed once more with authority when none other than his new *Führer der Unterseeboote*, Karl Dönitz, reprimanded him for using profanity during a gunnery exercise aboard *U 48*. However, beneath Dönitz's harsh words was an unspoken acknowledgement of Teddy's superb marksmanship and willingness to shave away the rigidity that sometimes marked the surface fleet in order to achieve whatever results were desired.

Under three successive commanders—each winning the Knight's Cross—and during twelve war patrols, *U 48* went on to become the most successful U-boat of the Second World War. Of the 300,000 tons that *U 48* destroyed at sea, Teddy had fired torpedoes accounting for over half of that total, a primary task of the First Watch Officer being torpedo shooting when the boat was engaged in a surface attack. On 3 November 1940, in recognition of this achievement, Teddy became the first Watch Officer to be awarded the Knight's Cross.[11]

The second man to captain *U 48*, Hans Rudolf Rösing, arrived in May 1940 as temporary relief for Herbert Schultze, incapacitated through illness. He had the advantage of being well acquainted with *U 48*, having commanded the 7th U-Flotilla since January:

Schultze had an excellent crew—one of the best I ever saw. When he fell seriously ill and couldn't go out, they needed another captain. So I was sent aboard *U 48* three or four days before leaving for the mission. Since I knew them all, it was no problem and I told them, 'Well, each sub has its customs. Leave it as it is, and if I don't like

something then I'll tell you.' But there was one thing we altered. My lucky number is seven and therefore I saw to it that any course we steered was divisible by seven, and I told my people that, although we had a command in the German Navy that meant 'ten degrees to port or ten degrees to starboard,' we would have a new command 'seven degrees to port'. It didn't mean anything, but these little things are important for the mood of the crew. . . . Suhren and [Otto] Ites, they followed my wishes, they understood. So we were a fine group, together with [Erich] Zürn, the engineer.

When we were waiting and sat in the mess on *U 48*, we played a child's game—*Fang den Hut* ['Catch the Hat', somewhat similar to Ludo]—because in war, of course, there were long periods of boredom interrupted with short periods of great anxiety. We never played cards. We talked together . . . we were in our little mess room a good gang—a happy crew.

Suhren was a very humorous man and extremely independent. Therefore you had to support him. If you left him alone, while giving him the support he needed, he was excellent. He was also an outstanding torpedo shot.

After two patrols with me on board [we] were one of the first boats to use Lorient. So I immediately telephoned Dönitz, and he said to me, 'You must leave the boat.' Well . . .I let him know that I was not of the same opinion. But of course it was important for him that I leave, because many of the older commanders, the experienced men from peacetime, had been killed. We were few, and he needed us for other commitments, so I was sent to the Italians in Bordeaux. I would have preferred to stay with so fine a crew: we were more than friends.[12]

The run of luck that had begun with Herbert Schultze continued under Rösing's command, Teddy viewing his new commander with great respect for his style of leadership and handling of what could have been a difficult crew for any officer who failed to gain their trust. The men aboard *U 48* were a tightly knit brotherhood that would not have tolerated fools in command. Heinrich Bleichrodt, an ex-merchant mariner, was *U 48*'s third commander, and it was under

In Germany it was common for a town or city to 'adopt' a U-boat—the so-called 'Patenschaft' scheme. U 564 was thus adopted by Zwei-brucken in the coal-mining Saarland region, and the crew would occasionally visit the town and receive the hospitality of its inhabitants. Here Suhren and part of his crew are pictured with local dignitaries on a visit during August 1941.

U 564 leads Kaptlt. Forster's U 654 into Lorient harbour during the morning of 10 July after their overnight voyage from Brest.

his leadership that Teddy received his Knight's Cross, Bleichrodt refusing to accept one awarded to him if Teddy did not receive the decoration in turn. In total, by October 1940, when Teddy departed the boat for commander training, U 48 had discharged 119 torpedoes in action—sixty-five of them fired by Teddy, of which thirty had hit the target.

In February 1941 U 564 was launched from Hamburg's huge Blohm & Voss shipyards, and Teddy was transferred aboard to take his first command, commissioned into the Kriegsmarine on 3 April 1941. As well as his soaring reputation, Teddy brought one further legacy from U 48—the boat's Wappen, an unofficial painting or symbol that graced the conning towers of almost all operational U-boats. For U 564, Teddy kept his old boat's character, a large black cat, its back arched above the characters '3X' and tail held high. In Germany, as in other countries, one black cat may be bad luck, but three will turn away misfortune. Soon the commander and crew sported their own smaller metal emblems on their caps and the newest dreimal schwarze Kater boat went to war.

A true maverick, Teddy is remembered even today as much for his continual clashes with authority and irrepressible sense of hum-our as for his gift for sub-marine warfare and leader-ship of men. The stories of his exploits ashore and almost constant reprimands equal those of his cool nerve in action, and have become almost legendary.

Fortunately for Teddy, in a nation where the frenetic activity of Reich security forces could condemn a man for the slightest slur cast upon the nation's leader-ship, Dönitz held a pro-

tective hand over the vast majority of his men, and over those he favoured in particular. Teddy had already been investigated by the *Abwehr* Intelligence Service for association with a Jewish woman, and drinking raucously with a black African man in a Hamburg bar. When confronted with the *Abwehr*'s four-page typewritten dossier, Dönitz's deputy, Admiral Hans-Georg von Friedeburg, disposed of it with the scribbled annotation 'complete rubbish' in the margin. Indeed, the entire issue of Aryan racial superiority was anathema to the young Teddy. After 6 September 1941 when Reinhard Heydrich's SS Security Office legislated that all German Jews were to wear the Star of David sewn on to the outside of their clothing, Teddy was perplexed after being confronted with the sight of several elderly

After an overnight stay as guests of the 2nd U-Boat Flotilla, both boats prepare to leave Lorient. At left is *U 654*, and the boat in the foreground is Teddy's *U 564*, her crew assembling for their formal evening departure.

Berliners in the Kurfürstendamm wearing the yellow cloth patch. He felt compelled to investigate:

Entirely naively, I asked one of the group what it meant. He looked at me in amazement.

'My dear sir, this is the Star of David which we are obliged to wear'.

That was still running through my mind when I sat down in a street café. Two members of the Hitler Youth crossed over to me. They wanted my autograph or something signing. I was pretty short with them and refused. It wasn't the young people who were to blame, and they were surprised and offended. So had I been, but for quite a different reason.[13]

At sea, five war patrols into the North Atlantic and along the American coast had accumulated a grim tally to Teddy's already impressive combat record, adding the Oak Leaves to his Knight's Cross in December 1941 and accelerating his promotion to *Kapitän-leutnant*:

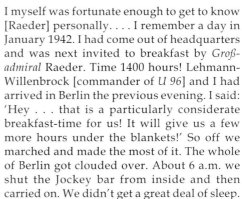

I myself was fortunate enough to get to know [Raeder] personally. . . . I remember a day in January 1942. I had come out of headquarters and was next invited to breakfast by *Groß-admiral* Raeder. Time 1400 hours! Lehmann-Willenbrock [commander of *U 96*] and I had arrived in Berlin the previous evening. I said: 'Hey . . . that is a particularly considerate breakfast-time for us! It will give us a few more hours under the blankets!' So off we marched and made the most of it. The whole of Berlin got clouded over. About 6 a.m. we shut the Jockey bar from inside and then carried on. We didn't get a great deal of sleep.

Then, at 1400 hours, breakfast started. The Admiral's staff smirked near us, and Raeder kept gasping for air so as not to be completely overcome by the intoxicating fumes as we were sitting not too far from him. Later, during a conversation over coffee and cognac, I could see that when Raeder was discussing non-functioning torpedoes with me he was trying to go into reverse in order to extricate himself from my alcoholic cloud. When, around 1600 hours, he excused himself and left his admirals to it, we all . . . sat down cosily round the table, and, among other things, negotiated my promotion to *Kapitän-leutnant*. . . . The next day I was supposed to get my U-boat badge with diamonds, and then the promotion was supposed to be announced by Raeder. I did indeed receive the U-boat badge, but no promotion, and as I

left the room of the *Oberbefehlshaber der Marine*, I met Admiral [Otto] Backenköhler, who congratulated me on my rise in rank. I said, 'No promotion. It didn't work out.' I had just about got to the bottom of the grand staircase nearby when *Kapitän* Freiwald [Raeder's adjutant] summoned me back, coat-tails flying. The *Oberbefehlshaber der Marine* said to me, 'Now you must submit to something else; I promote you to *Kapitänleutnant*.'

Behind him grinned Admiral Schulte-Montig, beside me Freiwald. I stood there and could hardly restrain a smile, and my face must have been even more stupid looking than usual, so that the *Oberbefehlshaber der Marine* . . . asked me, 'Well, don't you believe me? It's my prerogative; I can do it.'[14]

In early 1942 Teddy was at the zenith of his operational career, despite almost becoming the victim of a tragic accident during April.[15] Three days outbound from Brest on 7 April, in weather rated as 'still endurable' for Biscay (west-south-west Force 6 winds, with a swell of four metres), the boat's IWO, *LzS* Hans-Ferdinand Geisler, had enquired from the bridge watch on duty what was causing a loud and regular banging noise from the U-boat's upper deck. Believing it to be either a loose hatch or even a contraband stock of beer stashed beneath the wooden deck grating, Teddy ordered *Bootsmann* Heinz Webendörfer to proceed along the U-boat's slippery casing to investigate what indeed later transpired to be a damaged hatch cover.

Webendörfer was harnessed to the conning tower jumper wires as he began the perilous task of fastening the hatch, the U-boat frequently inundating him with rolling green water. While the unfortunate man clung to the bucking deck, Teddy arrived on the bridge to oversee the operation, without lifejacket or safety harness, and made the rash decision to help the struggling man.

As he peered over the rim of the conning tower, preparing to descend to the deck, *U 564* struck a towering wave. Webendörfer hung on for dear life as the steel hull was temporarily submerged. Teddy, however, was not quick enough, and, as the conning tower broke free of the swirling water, the cry '*Kommandant über Bord!*' echoed into the Control Room. Both engines were immediately thrown into full reverse as Teddy, now several metres away, desperately kicked off his cumbersome leather jacket (with heavy Zeiss binoculars and a Mauser pistol in its pockets), trousers and sea boots in an effort to stay afloat. Fortunately, the young commander was successfully retrieved from the water, clinging to a life-ring thrown from the U-boat's bridge. The only casualty of the event was Teddy's pride.

In a bizarre example of paper-driven military bureaucracy, there was an official enquiry into the event, and the loss of equipment from *U 564*. Suhren's list of items included '1 rain jacket (sou'wester), 1 three-quarter length leather jacket, 1 pair leather trousers, 1 pair U-boat boots (with cork soles), 1 Mauser pistol (7.65mm calibre), 1 artillery stopwatch, 1 pair of sunglasses in case, 1 artillery torch.'

Teddy's official statement—made in his inimitably tongue-in-cheek style—accompanied similar statements from Webendörfer and *Stabsobersteuermann* Limburg (IIIWO) for the enquiry, and concluded:

> One cannot blame *Bootsmann* Webendörfer that the commander climbed down on to the upper deck to help repair the damaged hatch cover. Furthermore, I do not consider *Bootsmann* Webendörfer to be responsible for what the commander carries in his pockets. All efforts to retrieve the lost items remained unsuccessful, and I should like to request that the lost items be replaced. [Signed] Suhren.

Dressed in his newly issued U-boat leathers, *PK Maat* Haring (left of photograph) talks to Rudolf ('Handsome Rudi') Meisinger in Lorient before *U 564*'s departure. Meisinger was another naval war correspondent, already a veteran of U-boat and minesweeper patrols.

Everything but the pistol and stopwatch were replaced by Brest's quartermaster department, and the entire report was circulated amongst the U-boat service by Karl Dönitz as part of a 'Humour in Wartime' series.

By mid-1942, Germany's U-boats seemingly teetered on the edge of Atlantic dominance, savaging the vulnerable trade routes that kept the United Kingdom's war effort from grinding to an irreversible standstill. Losses of Allied merchant shipping traffic had climbed inexorably since a brief respite during the previous December. This fearful predation culminated in June 1942's destruction by German U-boat of 130 ships — 613,682 tons of merchant shipping sent to the bottom worldwide, a figure that would be bettered only once more during the war. For the Germans. the tantalising scent of victory lay barely over the horizon; for the Allies, disaster loomed nearby as it finally began to appear possible that *Admiral* Karl Dönitz's vaunted 'Sea Wolves' might achieve their difficult goal.

The Allied advantage of having broken the U-boat's 'Enigma' code during most of 1941 had disappeared in February with the combined introduction of an improved cipher named 'Triton' and the four-rotor 'Enigma' machine. Bletchley Park would struggle with this new code until the year's end. On the other side of the hill' Germany's *B-Dienst* intelligence service had matched Allied code-breaking success concurrently, penetrating Naval Cipher No 3 that was used by the Royal, Royal Canadian and United States Navies within the Atlantic. At one point, Dönitz estimated that 50 per cent of his effective operational intelligence originated from *B-Dienst*, although it took years of combat before U-boat strength was able to fully capitalise on the intelligence bonanza.

However, intelligence alone could not fight the war. While convoy after convoy of crucial supplies and military material headed east across the Atlantic, more and more U-boats sailed to intercept and destroy. Exhorted by Dönitz (known to and beloved by German submariners as 'The Lion'), the 'Grey Wolves' attacked without pause. It was into this arena of combat that Teddy prepared to take his Type VIIC *U 564* in July 1942.

On 9 July, in the French port of Brest, where *U 564* was stationed as part of the 1st U-Boat Flotilla, the veteran crew geared up to put to sea once more, their destination on this occasion the balmy waters of the Caribbean. Theirs was to be one of ten boats despatched from Europe to the Western Atlantic waters edging the United States and Caribbean Sea, and it was *U 564*'s second journey to the region. It was also to be Teddy Suhren's last combat patrol before he rotated out of the front line to help train and shape the commanders of the future. Dönitz made his feelings plain when Teddy reported to BdU to be briefed on his forthcoming patrol:

Suhren, make sure you bring your boat safely back home and then come ashore. Then we can use you back at home for training. Prien, Kretschmer and Schepke would in theory have been ideal for the job, but they are all gone. Prien and Schepke are dead, Kretschmer a prisoner. [Erich] Topp has already come ashore—and you're next.[16]

On Friday 3 July 1942, *U 564* underwent dockyard tests to check her trim under water and verify the free movement of hydroplanes and rudders as well as ensuring the functionality of the echo-sounding installation. Rust treatment eliminated all traces of the corrosive effect of salt water along the steel hull and her external armaments, after which final preparatory work was undertaken on 5 July as the boat lay docked for refuelling, gallons of diesel flooding into her cavernous fuel bunkers. The following day it was time to arm the boat, and torpedoes and ammunition were embarked as *U 564* lay moored within the thick concrete shelter built on the Brest

shoreline. Provisions took a further two days to store, wedged into every nook and cranny that could accommodate either fresh or preserved foodstuffs. By Wednesday, the entire crew had been given medical examinations by Doctor Richter, Surgeon for the 1st U-Boat Flotilla, and the following evening, 9 July, after all fresh rations had been carefully stowed, *U 564* left Brest at 2130 hours alongside *Oberleutnant zur See* Ludwig Forster's *U 654*. Both boats followed the 'Herz' route through the lethal defensive minefields, bound for Lorient and escorted from harbour by two *Vorpostenboote* and a single *Sperrbrecher* as the combined threats of enemy aircraft and mines were very real. In Lorient, Teddy was ordered to take aboard a passenger.

Propaganda Kompanie Maat Haring was temporarily attached as a war correspondent to capture the cruise on camera of one of Germany's new generation of U-boat heroes. The naval branch of the *Propaganda Kompanie* was based in France, operating under the auspices of *KK* Karl Hinsch's *Marinekriegsberichterabteilung West* and frequently assigned to the U-boats, still wreathed in the glamour of an élite service. The officer directly commanding the correspondents aboard submarines was the noted journalist Wolfgang Frank, now famous for his books on the U-boat war and on Günther Prien in particular, written both during and after the conflict.

The U-boats were no strangers to the attentions of propaganda, frequently appearing within the pages of all manner of periodicals issued in Germany and the occupied countries. However, Teddy appeared almost to resent the intrusion aboard 'his' boat by Haring. Despite his outgoing exuberance, Teddy was uncomfortable beneath the glare of publicity, a fact remembered by Harald Busch, a correspondent who had been tasked with interviewing him during January 1942:

> Indeed, he seemed inhibited, as if he knew he was being watched. I had the impression that he was too clever to be able to relax and enjoy himself in his new-found position of fame. He did not like to allow himself to be praised by a public with whom as a U-boat man he was not likely to have much in common. Of course, he was proud to have achieved successes, but he was unable to put on an act before people who belonged to a quite different society, who would have no comprehension of his own. Reinhard Suhren seemed to me to be an unusually reflective man, who liked to conceal the fact, very much beneath the comic antics of a clown: 'Come on children, don't look so worried! Don't take yourselves so seriously!' That was how he seemed to me, and he was having to leave the circus specially for me, because I had come to annoy him with my order to find out all about him.[17]

Thus, in early July 1942, Haring joined the crew of *U 564*, given no special duties aboard the boat other than to make himself generally useful and not get in the way. His primary 'weapons' were a small cine-camera and a Leica for taking still photographs with which he would record the daily life of one of Germany's veteran submarines.

It would be Saturday 11 July before both boats finally left France, sailing under similar escort as before from Lorient into the Bay of Biscay, following the swept 'Kernleder' route. At the channel's end, 'Point Kern', two hours' cruising west from Lorient, a final flashed 'Good hunting' from the small patrol ships and their larger *Sperrbrecher* cousin heralded the end of their anti-aircraft and minesweeping escort, the surface vessels turning back leaving the two U-boats to thunder alone towards the Atlantic. *U 564*'s bridge lookouts soon lost sight of Forster's boat in the deepening twilight. Presently they would begin the deadly routine of alternate stalking and hiding as the 'Three Black Cats' proceeded west into the Atlantic killing grounds.

1 Outbound

11–16 JULY

U 564 departs Lorient, travelling behind Forster's *U 654*.

AFTER drifting gradually out of contact with one another, the two boats sailed westwards along parallel courses. Upon reaching the deep-water curve that mirrored the sweep of Brittany's granite coastline, they both submerged in their first operational test dives to check seals, trim and onboard systems. The faint hum of *U 654*'s distant propellers turning gently under electric power receded until Teddy's boat was once more isolated within the turbulent waters of the Bay of Biscay. Weeks of leave in Germany and the recreation centres of Paris and Brittany faded to distant memories as the mainly veteran men fell swiftly into their familiar duties and work patterns aboard the boat.

Experience often marked the difference between survival and death for the precarious existence of Germany's 'Grey Wolves', and *U 564* was fortunate to have a predominantly tried and tested crew. Forty-four men — plus their passenger from the *Propaganda Kompanie* — comprised the complement of Teddy's boat as she departed France, twenty-nine of them having served aboard since *U 564*'s April 1941 commissioning.

Of the four permanent officers on board, the irrepressibly good-humoured IIWO, *LzS* Herbert Waldschmidt ranked as probably the most inexperienced. This twenty-year-old Dortmund native had joined the boat in March 1942 and had been to sea with Teddy on the boat's previous cruise, *U 564* his first taste of submarine combat after graduating from the officer crew of XII/1939. That

patrol, stretching from April to early June 1942, provided Teddy with the most successful Type VII voyage of May, claiming 35,000 tons of shipping sunk (an unintentional overclaim because two of his believed victims were only in fact damaged, and later towed to repair yards).[1] However, his most unfortunate and significant victim was the 4,000-ton Mexican tanker SS *Petrero del Llano*, attacked and destroyed with torpedoes near Sands Key, Florida. Teddy maintained that the ship had been travelling under armed escort and blacked out, while the Mexican Government remained adamant that searchlights had been trained on to huge Mexican flags emblazoned along her superstructure. With thirteen crewmen killed in the attack, the pro-Allied government declared war against Germany on 22 May. It was to mark a fresh U-boat onslaught as Dönitz subsequently lifted restrictions against Mexican shipping in the Gulf of Mexico.

Waldschmidt's responsibilities as the boat's IIWO were related primarily to the artillery aboard—both deck and flak weapons—as well as to some of the more mundane administrative matters. Combined with duty at the head of two of the day's six watches atop the conning tower, he decided when the U-boat's surface weapons required cleaning to ensure their readiness for action at all times. He was also often obliged to decode particular classified messages transmitted from the BdU, other, routine radio traffic being left to the experienced communications teams led by non-commissioned officers Rudi Elkerhausen and Willi Anderheyden.

Waldschmidt had melded well with his new crew, as had his immediate superior, IWO *ObltzS* Ulf Lawaetz, who had also come aboard during the same period. But, unlike Waldschmidt, Lawaetz had tasted action before joining the U-boat service. Christened Ulf Erling Günther Lawaetz, he had been born in Copenhagen in 1916 to a Danish engineer who worked within German shipyards, and a German mother. The first of five siblings, Ulf was a student at Denmark's Sorø Akademi before beginning cadet training as a *Sökadet Ældste Klasse* in the Royal Danish Navy. It was in 1937, at the age of 21 and three years after the premature death of his mother, that he was compelled to choose between Danish or German citizenship, and correspondingly between a vocation in the German or Danish Navies. His Danish naval superiors advised him to leave his country of birth and go to Germany to enrol in the *Kriegsmarine* if he was at all serious about a naval career. At that time, Denmark's government was pacifist by nature, and the chances of a military profession in Denmark were extremely slim. So it was that Lawaetz opted for German citizenship, graduating soon afterwards as an officer from the *Kriegsmarine* Crew of 37b. Subsequently he was posted to the destroyer *Hans Lüdemann* (*Z 18*) as Second Artillery Officer in November 1939 as the war entered its third month.

The Bridge Watch—and sightseers. Heinz Mattern, the electric motor *Obermaschinist*, is at left, while at the extreme right is *Funkmaat* Willi Anderheyden; neither is a member of the watch. Second from right is *Oberbootsmann* Heinz Webendörfer, of the First Watch. The other, less visible members of this four-man watch were IWO Ulf Lawaetz, Ernst Schlittenhard and Eduard Kalbach.

In April 1940, as Germany's Operation 'Weserübung' burst upon Norway, *Hans Lüdemann* was amongst those destroyers earmarked to carry mountain troops to the distant northern port of Narvik. There, after unloading its precious cargo of troops and equipment, Lawaetz's destroyer was one of the squadron of ten that were all lost. With two sunk on 10 April and one damaged beyond repair, the remaining seven, including *Hans Lüdemann*, were taken by surprise in a bold attack mounted by the battleship HMS *Warspite* and escorting Royal Navy destroyers three days later. U-boats, positioned to screen the German surface ships, were powerless to protect them, their torpedoes without exception malfunctioning as they attempted to intercept the incoming threat. After a brief and fierce struggle, all ten German destroyers were sunk, Lawaetz among the bedraggled men who dragged themselves ashore only to find themselves embroiled in the bitter infantry war as Allied forces and the German mountain troops wrestled for control of the battered city. He became a part of the improvised naval infantry regiment soon named the *Gebirgs-marine* (Mountain Navy) by their Army comrades. Eventually, with an Allied evacuation,

the Germans prevailed and the shipwrecked survivors of the sunken destroyers were rotated home to more orthodox naval assignments.

Lawaetz, for rather obvious reasons, was posted to the *Marine-befehlshaber* Denmark, where his knowledge of the local language and customs were considered extremely useful, before being once more transferred as Second Artillery Officer to the heavy cruiser (and former 'pocket-battleship') *Lützow* in March 1941 (at the time, the ship was still in the yards after being torpedoed by HMS *Spearfish*). Six months later, Lawaetz was back in Scandinavia as part of Helsinki's Marine Attaché staff before, in September 1941, he volunteered for Dönitz's élite. He swiftly began U-boat training and was within a short while posted to *U 564* to replace *ObltzS* Hans-Ferdinand Geisler as IWO.[2]

The forward torpedo compartment at evening suppertime. Crowded and uncomfortable, this single compartment housed upwards of twenty-five men, crammed into the twelve bunks. The *Mechanikermaat*, Gerhard Ehlers, had his own bunk; the remaining crew made the best that they could of the available space.

As the U-boat's executive officer, Lawaetz was essentially the second-in-command, and responsible for maintenance of the boat's torpedo armament, as well as for the first watch of each day and a second four-hour shift starting at 1200 hours. In regard to his torpedo duty, his task was to maintain the submarine's main weapon and all of its complex fire control systems in peak readiness for action. However, the actual maintenance of the torpedoes themselves was not Lawaetz's responsibility, that duty being assumed by Gerhard Ehlers, the boat's *Mechanikermaat*, or Chief Torpedo Mate. However, when the boat was used for surface attacks, the firing of the torpedoes was the domain of the IWO, under the close supervision of the boat's commander, who exercised supreme control atop the tower, maintaining an all-round picture while the IWO could concentrate on shooting.

Teddy's gifted Chief Engineer (*Lietender Ingenieur*, or LI), Berliner *Oblt (Ing.)* Ulrich Gabler, was a highly qualified maritime designer and had been involved in ship construction before the war. Born in 1913, Gabler had studied shipbuilding in Berlin-Charlottenburg before becoming an assistant to Professor Schnadel at the Ingenieur-kontor für Schiffbau company in Lübeck. Following his call-up to the naval reserves in 1939, he joined the U-boat service and became LI aboard the Type II training boat *U 121*. Once assigned to *U 564*, before the new boat had begun construction, he personally attended each step of her manufacture, becoming familiar with every frame and rivet of the new Type VIIC as she took shape in Hamburg's famous Blohm & Voss yards. The working relationship between Gabler and Suhren was excellent, and after five war patrols together the two men were also firm friends. During June, when *U 564* had returned from her action off the coast of Florida, Gabler had been due to come ashore and be posted to U-boat research, but Teddy had consulted with Dönitz and point-blank refused to sail without him. The headstrong commander predictably declined to give ground on the matter, and Gabler's transfer ashore was deferred for one more patrol.

Gabler's position as Chief Engineer placed him on virtually an equal footing with Suhren when it came to the operation of *U 564*. His duties as head of the boat's technical crew comprised the complete mechanical control of the boat, particularly her crucial diving and propulsion systems. A good relationship between LI and commander was essential for the boat's success, and, in the partnership of Suhren and Gabler, *U 564* had as good as it could possibly get. While the commander had two Watch Officers to assist him with many of his responsibilities, the LI had two senior non-commissioned officers answering directly to him, one accountable for the diesel engines the other for the electric motors and their respective crews.

Gabler was joined on his final patrol by another engineering officer, *Leutnant der Reserve (Ing.)* Eberhard Hammermüller, assigned by U-Boat Command to accompany a front-line boat into action in order to gain combat experience from a veteran chief engineer. As an extra body aboard an already crowded boat, Hammermüller bedded down in the *Unteroffizier* room, sharing the confined space with the boat's *Maate*.

The remainder of the crew sailing for the Atlantic aboard *U 564* in July 1942 were mainly old hands at submarine warfare, and represented a typical cross-section of German sailors. Their geographical homes ranged from Wilhelmshaven on the North Sea coast to Triften, a small village less than 20 kilometres from the German/Austrian border. Likewise, the crew ranged in age from 18-year-old *Matrosengefreiter* Paul Stephan, already a veteran of a single patrol aboard *U 564*, to *Stabsobersteuermann* Karl Limburg, who was 43.

Limburg, nicknamed 'Stürkorl' (an old low-German sailing-ship term for helmsman, although remembered by Herbert Waldschmidt as being derived from *Steuer*, meaning helm, being added to his Christian name of Karl), had even seen service in the *Kaiser*'s Navy during the First World War, when he had earned the Iron Cross

In this series of mealtime photographs, the floor is covered with two torpedoes, provisions and mattresses, and the lower level of bunks is folded out of the way to make room for the 'eels', leaving even less space available. The bunks that the men are leaning against are the top row. Collapsible tables were available, stored under the lower bunks and completely impractical without access to the deck.

The bread that accompanies the meal was one of the first items in the provisions list to spoil during a patrol. Soon, once the outsides had moulded completely, the men would be reduced to scooping out and eating the stale insides only. After that, too, had become inedible, canned bread was used. In the photograph lower right are *Matrosengefreiter* Eduard Kalbach and Roland Schiedhelm (pouring coffee). This was Kalbach's first trip aboard *U 564*.

Second Class. Entering the *Kaiserliche Marine* at the age of fifteen as war broke out in 1914, Limburg served throughout the four devastating years of conflict that followed, staying in naval service during the difficult period after the end of hostilities when the Navy's honour was considered stained by revolution in 1918. He left the military in 1928, only to re-join immediately when a new European war broke out eleven years later. Limburg was the most senior of the non-commissioned officers aboard. As *Stabsobersteuermann*, he was also the boat's IIIWO and responsible for the third slot of the three daily watches. Administratively, Limburg exercised control over where and how provisions were stored aboard the boat, liaising with Gabler so as to be able to provide an accurate report of weight displacement for the boat's successful trimming. But his main function was as navigator, and it was he who plotted the boat's course, whether transiting the Atlantic or giving chase to enemy convoy traffic. Teddy also made one concession to Limburg as the oldest man aboard: he allowed him a personal supply of rum to ease what were often aching joints from the confinement of U-boat life. At the end of the boat's first war patrol in 1941, Limburg had confessed to 'tapping off' his own supply of the boat's stored medicinal rum, blaming breakage for the sudden decrease in volume before Teddy managed to drag a confession from him. The matter was soon solved with Teddy's compromise solution, demonstrating the commander's ability at man-management that marked him as a popular and effective captain.

Teddy had carefully managed to keep a hard core of his original crew together at a time when many other veteran crews were broken up and posted elsewhere to provide experienced cadres for newly commissioned U-boats. A bare sprinkling of new sailors were distributed throughout *U 564*, the young men eager to begin their first patrol and become part of the comradeship earned only through days spent at sea.

The men quickly adapted to the rhythm of shipboard life, whether new to the motions of a medium-size U-boat or one of the old hands. The watch rotation aboard *U 564* consisted of four-hour shifts for virtually all but the engine and motor personnel, who worked six hours at a stretch. The radio crew also shared this longer period on duty during the 'graveyard shift' of what was usually a reduced volume of radio traffic. To keep some kind of normality and firm structure to an already difficult environment, the boat time remained fixed at German Summer Time, i.e. two hours ahead of Greenwich Mean Time. In this way, for example, breakfast was served always in the 'morning', whatever time of day local clocks would show.

U 564 was a Type VIIC, the workhorse of the U-Boat Service and a model present in nearly every theatre of war in which the *Kriegsmarine* was involved. Type VIIs ranged from the frozen wastes of the Arctic to equatorial Africa and the Americas, travelling distances that their designers had never originally envisaged and proving deadly and capable war machines. At first, the Type VIIC was considered too small to cross the Atlantic from France to the United States, and that task was left for the larger Type IX U-boats. The normal surfaced range for a Type VIIC travelling at 10 knots of 8,500 nautical miles (extended by using a combined diesel and electric drive to 9,700 nautical miles) would have allowed only a limited time at best around the central western Atlantic, with little by way of fuel reserve to allow the boat a margin of safety for its return.

However, it was found that the crew were prepared to make their difficult and uncomfortable tenure aboard the VIICs even more harsh, replacing quantities of fresh water with fuel and cramming every possible provision aboard so that their torpedoes could be added to the escalating war against America. *U 564* benefited from the presence of Gabler, with his vast knowledge of U-boat design and capabilities, while all U-boats profited during 1942 from the presence of a new addition to the U-boat war—the *Milchkuh* (Milk Cow) U-tanker. The first of these enormous submarines had embarked on her inaugural mission in March 1942, and when *U 564* ploughed through Biscay, two *Milchkühe* were also heading to their mid-Atlantic stations and three more were soon to put to sea.

Although Teddy was under orders to refuel from one such tanker before entering the Caribbean battleground, as *U 564* sailed from France she was stocked to capacity with stores for the forty-five men aboard. Fresh and canned food was hung or stashed in almost every available space. As with others of her class, food and ammunition took precedence aboard the sleek grey hull of the VIIC; considerations of crew comfort were minimal at best.

At the bow, the graceful taper of the outer deck casing extended nine metres past the end of the pressure hull, this free flooding casing, crowned with hardwood decking, giving the submarine's distinctive shape. Four bow torpedo tubes comprised the main teeth of the boat, and these extended nearly four metres into the pressure hull, where the bulk of the crew worked and lived for the duration of their voyage. This main weaponry dominated the forward torpedo room (*Bugraum*, or, bow-room). It was here that the enlisted men of the crew—the 'Lords'—lived alongside the massive cylindrical 'eels':

(Left to right) Werner Rieckhoff, Herman Hausruckinger, Werner Grünert, Ewald Gaiser, Werner Schlägel—the 'Lords' of the Torpedo Room.

over twenty-five sailors were accommodated within this compartment, sharing twelve bunks between them. Their roles at sea ranged from ship's cook, helmsmen, radio crew, torpedo mixers and stokers (a term hardly befitting U-boat engineers, but a traditional hangover from steam-powered naval vessels) to general sea duties, which could include standing watch or manning the flak and artillery. Stowage was minimal within the bow room, and extra clothing for each man normally was limited to little more than spare underwear. Only one person within the compartment had permanent access to a bunk, *Mechanikermaat* Gerhard Ehlers, the Torpedo Mate and sole petty officer to share the enlisted men's quarters:

> Life for the crew in the bow room was hard. When we left port we had four torpedoes in the tubes, four torpedoes in the bilge and two torpedoes above the bilge, so that in the bow room we had ten torpedoes altogether. The two torpedoes above the bilge were covered with sheets of wood. On those they had to eat, and also the bunks were there. Right above them was the scaffolding (girders on which torpedoes were hoisted for loading and maintenance), meaning that the people hardly had room to move about, and if they did, they were often on all fours! Even if the sea were reasonably calm, you always had the odd wave rocking the boat — and the pea soup went everywhere![3]

Through a narrow doorway and immediately abaft the forward torpedo room was the forward head, the small toilet attached to the port bulkhead, with an equally small food storage locker opposite to starboard. Abaft again of these small cubicles, the next section was slightly more spacious. This was the *Oberfeldwebelraum* (Chief Petty Officer's room), and here the senior non-commissioned officers shared the four bunks available, two on each side of the slim passageway. A small drop-leaf table was also provided, slightly offset to port. *Diesel Obermaschinist* Hermann Kräh, *Elektro Obermaschinist* Heinz Mattern, *Bootsmann* Heinz Webendörfer and *Stabsobersteuermann* Limburg occupied this room. Webendörfer, turned twenty-six during June, was the crew chief aboard *U 564*. His primary role was to maintain discipline and order among the enlisted personnel for the smooth running of the boat. Known to the crew as 'Number One', he was also responsible for the crew's clothing and equipment, as well as for the general cleanliness of the boat itself. Kept permanently busy by his wealth of duties, Webendörfer held the authority to deal with any disciplinary matters before they required the attention of ranking officers. He also took his part in watch-keeping, attached to Lawaetz's first watch. During attacks he was stationed within the conning tower, where he input the information relayed verbally from either Suhren's or Lawaetz's targeting into the boat's torpedo computer, from where it was electrically transmitted straight to the

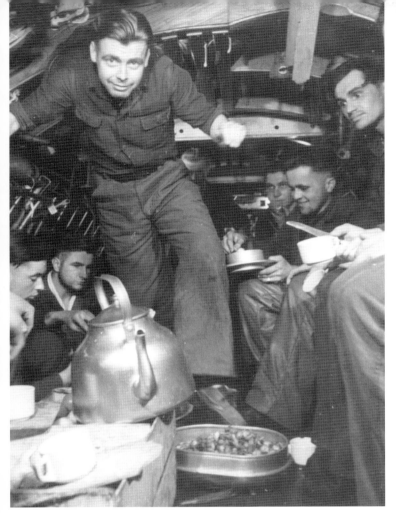

'eels' within their tubes. Weben-dörfer was in turn supported in his tasks by two other *Maate*, *Oberbootsmannsmaat* Heinrich Bartels and *Bootsmannsmaat* Karl-Ernst Thiel. As well as assisting with discipline and the crew's well-being, Bartels was charged with maintaining and recording all the ammunition stowed aboard *U 564* (with the exception of the torpedoes), while Thiel attended to the 8.8cm deck cannon and to the administrative and personnel concerns of the boat's seamen.

Past the *Oberfeldwebelraum* was the *Offizierraum* (Officer's Room). Here the pressure hull nearly reached its widest point (4.7 metres in diameter), the officer's bunks set slightly back from the main passageway. A small table to port doubled as a wardroom. It was on the seats here that Gabler slept, a folding bunk above

Mechanikermaat Ehlers — the only petty officer to bunk in the forward torpedo room — threads his precarious way to the Petty Officer's Mess (*Unteroffizier Raum*) for his own meal. Behind and around him (left to right) are Wagner, Becker, Rieckhoff, Hausruckinger and Grünert.

him available for his use but barely used. Opposite, to starboard, the First and Second Watch Officers, Ulf Lawaetz and Herbert Waldschmidt, slept. Four small wardrobes crowded the compartment but allowed crucial room for storing the officers' scant belongings that were permitted on board.

The next stage abaft the wardroom was given over to the only semi-private area aboard. On the port side of the passage was the commander's quarters. Separated from the rest of the boat by a heavy green felt curtain, Teddy had a small desk and his own bunk, from where he could listen to the activity aboard. The two most important information-gathering areas were directly opposite him. To starboard, a rotating watch of pairs from the four-man radio crew constantly manned both the *Horchraum* (listening room), with its *Gruppen-Horch-Gerät* (GHG) hydrophone equipment, and the small *Funkraum* (Radio Room). The GHG hydrophone incorporated eleven small receivers embedded in each side of the U-boat's bow in an arc, its open side at the bottom. An electric pulse-timing mechanism recorded the time differences that it took for sound impulses to reach the various individual receivers, acting as a basic form of directional indicator for the headphone-wearing operator within the listening compartment. This system had replaced the more accurate *Kristall-Basisgerät* (KDB) apparatus, a swivel hydrophone mounted above decks near the forward retractable bollards. However, although the KDB system offered a higher degree of precision, its range was substantially less than that of the GHG, which in optimum conditions could detect a single ship at a little over ten nautical miles and massed convoy traffic at fifty-four.

The *Funkraum* also sported what has become in later years one of the most famous aspects of the U-boat struggle within the Atlantic. The radio crew aboard *U 564* had been issued a brand new four-rotor 'Enigma' machine at the beginning of the year. Upon the outbreak of World War Two in 1939, the *Wehrmacht* possessed one of the most sophisticated military communication systems in the world. At the heart of this was the ability to transmit and receive secure coded messages via a supposedly unbreakable cryptographic machine, the original three-wheeled *Kriegsmarine* version of which was known as *Schlüsselmaschine M* (Code Writer M). These electro-

(Below) The petty officers' accommodation at mealtimes. This small area doubled as a mess, sporting two folding tables slightly offset to starboard. Eight bunks provided accommodation for the boat's *Maate*, their steward for meals being drawn from the enlisted men. As can be seen in the photographs, eating in the central companionway was prone to constant interruption. Seated around the tables from left to right are: *ObMaschmt* Fritz Stocker, *Maschmt* Hans Neumann, *ObMaschmt* Fritz Hummel, *Fkmt* Rudi Elkerhausen, *ObMaschmt* Emil Grade, *Btsmt* Heinrich Bartels and *Mechmt* Gerhard Ehlers. In the stern-facing photograph (left), the door to the small galley is at the compartment's far end.

 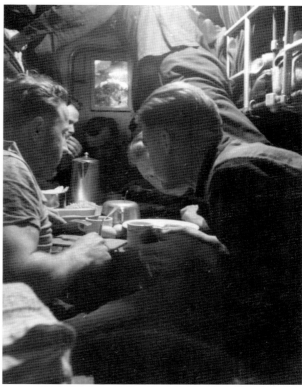

(Above) The difficulties of relaxing within such a confined space are amply demonstrated by this series of photographs. The companionway that traversed the Petty Officers' Room (*Unteroffizierraum*) was an important thoroughfare for virtually the entire crew, situated as it was between the bow room ratings' accommodation and the engine and motor rooms.

mechanical coding devices, resembling small portable typewriters, relied on a variable internal wiring and rotor system to provide an incredible 6,000,000,000 possible code settings, which were then changed daily.

While the British code-breakers at Bletchley Park's top secret Government Codes and Cipher School had managed to make some penetration into *Luftwaffe* and *Heer* 'Enigma' ciphers as early as 1939 (with enormous, and often overlooked, help from Polish crypt-analysts, who had been working on cracking the 'Enigma' for years both before the war and later in England), the more complex *Kriegs-marine* system defied early attempts at penetration. Various captures of single rotors from sinking U-boats and prisoners of war during the initial months of hostilities provided pieces for the complex jigsaw, but the first real breakthrough for British cryptanalysts came after an Allied raid in March 1940 on the Lofoten Islands, where the last of the series of eight rotors was captured from the *Vorpostenboot Krebs*, enabling Bletchley Park to decrypt some naval 'Enigma signals — albeit still with delays — from May onwards. The capture by a boarding party from the destroyer HMS *Somali* of an intact 'Enigma' codebook and rotors from the auxiliary supply/weather-

reporting ship *München* near Jan Mayen Island on 7 May 1940 added yet further to the British code-breaking ability. While this enabled the penetration of the low-grade weather code, it did not, however, aid access to the more complicated systems used by *Kriegsmarine* combat units such as destroyers and U-boats. But it was the seizure of an intact machine with all of its rotors and code books from *Kaptlt.* Fritz-Julius Lemp's *U 110* on 9 May 1941 that finally provided the key to unlock the U-boat 'Enigma'.

However, always suspicious that the 'Enigma' had been compromised, in late 1941 Dönitz introduced the new four-rotor coding machine which, after entering general service by February 1942, 'blacked out' Allied code-breakers with its new, massive range of variables. This, combined with a refined code-net named 'Triton' (known to the Allies as 'Shark') that came into use during the previous October, ensured that, for the rest of

(Above left) Second *Funkmaat* Willi Anderheyden on duty within the Radio Room. Anderheyden was a veteran U-boat crewman, having served on *Kapitänleutnant* Georg Wilhelm Schulz's *U 124*—the 'Edelweiss boat'—where he received the Iron Cross Second Class in October 1940. Signals traffic was heavy by the very nature of Dönitz's tight operational control of his boats and required constant monitoring. The Radio Room doubled as entertainment centre; beneath Anderheyden's out-stretched right arm is the boat's gramophone. The large receiver visible to the upper right is the U-boat's main Telefunken Type E 436S, covering frequencies between 3 and 30MHz. There was a small radio for commercial broadcasts as well. The voicepipe running to the bridge can be seen attached to the U-boat rib frame.

(Above right) This photograph of Anderheyden at work clearly shows the newly introduced four-rotor 'Enigma' machine. After its introduction during the early months of 1942, its new revised system net—codenamed 'Triton', or 'Shark' to the Allies—proved impenetrable to Allied code-breakers throughout most of that year.

1942, U-boat ciphers were impenetrable — and the Allies would suffer accordingly.[4]

Oberfunkmaat Rudi Elkerhausen headed the radio crew aboard *U 564*. *Funkobergefreiter* Werner Apitz supported him during duty period, while *Oberfunkmaat* Willi Anderheyden and *Funkobergefreiter* Ewald Gaiser handled the alternating watch. The radio was manned at all times, for four-hour periods for each watch during peak times (0800 to 2000 hours) and six hours outside of those times — even at periscope depth, where radio traffic could still be received. Of course, while one man on duty attended the radio transmitter and receiver, the other would take control of the hydrophone, sweeping the ocean for tell-tale signs of the enemy.

Abaft the cramped forward accommodation was a heavy, water-tight hatch that could seal off the boat's bow half in case of flooding. This circular hatch led directly to the *Zentrale* — the amidships section and nerve centre. The navigation periscope, helm, planes, blowing panel and numerous other systems were located here, as was the small navigation area. A metal ladder led upwards into the conning tower, which housed the attack periscope and TDC along with a secondary helm used for surfaced running, before leading to the

round main entry and exit hatch for the submarine's interior. One of only four external hatches, it was generally the only one in use while at sea, the main exceptions to this being occasions of stern and bow torpedo loading.

Both Gabler and Limburg were often to be found on duty within the Control Room, as was the boat's *Zentralemaat, Maschinenobermaat* Emil Grade, handling the fine adjustments of trim while submerged and the balance of air supply within the boat and maintaining the periscopes and their hydraulic lifting systems. Grade was assisted by any of three *Maschinenobergefreitern*, Johann Rebahn, Werner Rieckhoff or Hans Merk.

Past the *Zentrale*, another circular, pressure-tight hatch led to the compartment containing the *Unteroffizierraum* (Petty Officer Quarters). Eight bunks were used by the eleven petty officers in rotation, two folding

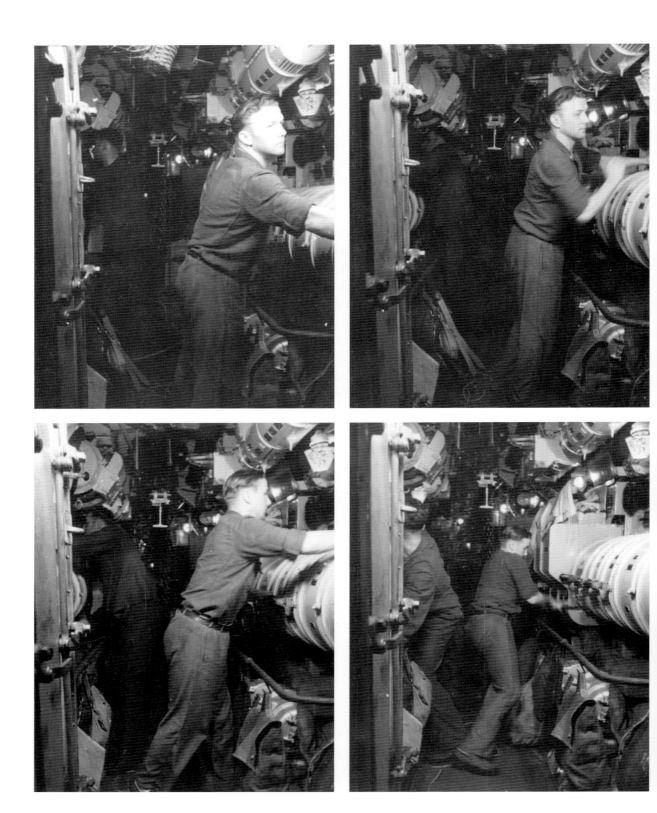

drop-leaf tables offset to starboard available for meals. Among the men who lived within this narrow compartment, its gangway in almost constant use, were Elkerhausen, Anderheyden, Bartels and Thiel, as well as seven more petty officers responsible for various aspects of the U-boat's propulsion systems. Additionally, *Leutnant (Ing.)* Eberhard Hammermüller and *PK Maat* Haring quartered for the duration of the voyage within this section.

The tiny galley was immediately abaft the *Unteroffizierraum*, a three-ring electric hob and two small ovens being all that *Matrosenobergefreiter* Hermann Hausruckinger had to work with in order to satisfy the ration requirements of the entire crew. Hausruckinger had been with the boat since her commissioning and had previously served as 'second cook' to Heinrich Ranm, before Ranm had been posted elsewhere. Now, as the boat's *Smutje* (cook), he was excused watch duties in order to concentrate on the almost constant demand for food or coffee by the alternating watches, although he often helped in general seamanship whenever available and wherever needed.

> The diet for the first eight days was quite good. For instance, we had a lot of fresh vegetables, fruit and so on. In fact everything fresh was used up first.
>
> The galley was between the *Unteroffizierraum* and the diesel room. Its cooker was on the port side, and on starboard there was a toilet, piled up with fresh vegetables, fruit, meat etc. First of all, it is not nice to have a toilet in the galley, but on the other hand, forty-six men to one toilet (in the bow half) is not enough!
>
> The biggest problem was the bread. We placed it into a hammock so that plenty of air could get to it, but after a while it used to go stale and [the loaves] looked like rabbits because they were covered in mildew. We just removed as much of it as possible and then ate it.
>
> When all the fresh food was used up, we turned to tinned food. On the whole, our provisions were very good; in fact we had everything—except it all tasted of diesel oil.[5]

Two geared, centrifugally supercharged Germaniawerft 6-cylinder, 4-stroke M6V 40/46 diesels dominated the next compartment, where sweating engineers nursed the thundering engines that provided surface propulsion for *U 564*. The engine-room crew worked six-hour shifts, divided into port and starboard watches. With ignition provided by compressed air from small tanks located outboard of the engine foundations, the powerful diesels could give slightly over seventeen knots if pushed to the absolute maximum. Further aft again, and separated by a slim doorway, was the final compartment. Here the smaller pair of BBC (Brown Boveri & Cie) electric motors were aligned along the propeller shafts to drive the U-boat while submerged. This elongated compartment also housed an emergency helm and the final single stern torpedo tube, a solitary reload hidden in the bilge beneath deck plating.

Within the bilge that ran the length of the boat there was almost as much space below as above the decking. However, it was given over to trim and diving tanks and the enormous banks of two 62-cell batteries, capable of producing 9,160 amp hours. These batteries provided the life-blood energy for the electric motors, but also comprised the Second World War U-boats' Achilles' heel. By the very nature of stored energy, they could soon be exhausted. Thus *U 564*, like all her sister-boats, could dive and operate on electric motors for only a limited time, and at a greatly reduced speed. Even at maximum revolutions, the electric motors could push *U 564* at little more than seven knots, a rate that would soon discharge the batteries completely. If the batteries were ever exhausted, the commander would be faced with two dire choices: surface and face whatever enemy lay in wait, or allow the propellers to cease rotating and the

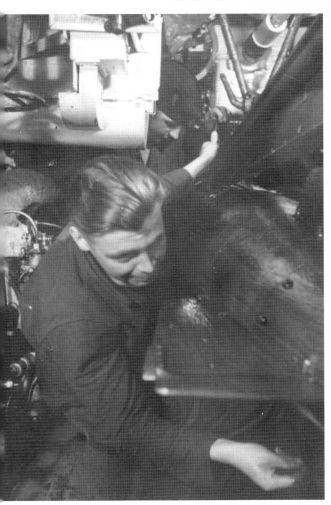

Mechanikermaat Gerhard Ehlers and *Mechankergefreiter* Horst Becker (with cap) service the stern torpedo. Torpedoes required constant attention and servicing to ensure reliability, Ehlers and his two torpedo mechanics being tasked with this maintenance. The floor of the stern compartment appears to be crowded with provisions—there are sacks of potatoes cluttering the deck.

U-boat to drop silently into the abyss until the pressure hull could no longer withstand the enormous weight of seawater and collapsed. In truth, the U-boat was more of a submersible than a submarine.

As *U 564* headed into the Bay of Biscay, the test dive proved her to be seaworthy and ready for action. Satisfied, Teddy ordered his boat surfaced beneath a moonless night sky. Diesel travel allowed *U 564* to make the best economical use of the boat's speed towards the main Atlantic, hastening across Biscay, which had become the domain of Allied anti-submarine aircraft. With easily identifiable 'choke points' of U-boat traffic entering and exiting the French Atlantic bases, Royal Air Force Coastal Command had stepped up its ASW patrols. For Dönitz, the threat they posed had begun to grow acute, and, in a Paris conference on 16 June, BdU and various OKM department heads held consultations to discuss U-boat anti-aircraft strategy for

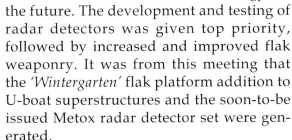

the future. The development and testing of radar detectors was given top priority, followed by increased and improved flak weaponry. It was from this meeting that the *'Wintergarten'* flak platform addition to U-boat superstructures and the soon-to-be issued Metox radar detector set were generated.

However, these issues were still in the future as *U 564* sailed west. Lookouts strained their eyes, attempting to penetrate the darkness for signs of hostile intruders. With an almost certain inevitability, the first such enemy was sighted at 0458 hours on 12 July, less than 100 nautical miles from Lorient. The ominous hum of British engines heralded the darkened shape of a bomber passing over the U-boat's wake, only 100 metres distant. Crewmen manned the small MG 34 machine gun as the large shadow swept by, its own weapons clearly visible, bristling from Perspex turrets. But this time there was no combat: the plane vanished as swiftly as it had come. 'Assume spotter plane that didn't see us because of the dark moonless night.'[6] Knowing that the chances of a second lucky escape were slim at best, Teddy took *U 564*

It was not just torpedoes that required regular attention and maintenance. With frequent submergence, there was a strong risk of corrosion and malfunction of the 8.8cm deck cannon. Thick coats of grease were applied whenever necessary. Here *Bootsmaat* Karl-Ernst Thiel and Suhren, who began his U-boat career as an artillery officer, are working on the weapon's starboard sighting mechanism. The delicate sight itself was detachable, and was usually removed prior to diving.

down at 0610 hours, and the rest of the morning was spent in the cradle of the deep, surfacing only with full daylight, when it was possible to observe greater distances in the clear summer visibility.

The following night, a repeat of the same experience sent *U 564* hurtling below, this time the watch crashing to the steel deck plates in an emergency dive. A Sunderland, the huge 'Tractor' as the Germans knew it, had homed unerringly on to the strongly phosphorescent wake that now plagued *U 564*, but it was foiled in its attack by the vigilant German lookouts. Once again the boat was forced to skulk westwards underwater at the feeble speed conferred by her electric motors, the risks of aerial attack outweighing any advantage of a speedy crossing. Even dawn brought little relief. The boat surfaced, and the crew hauled the MG 34 to its conning-tower mount, only to be brought plunging underwater again by the appearance of enemy aircraft less than twenty minutes later. It was an arduous process that rasped at the crew's raw nerves and brought into stark relief the growing threat of enemy aircraft.

Although, once free of the Biscay approaches, Teddy finally managed to proceed south-west for three uninterrupted days, elsewhere the aerial menace claimed its first victim from the ten westbound boats. Knight's Cross holder Gerhard Bigalk's *U 751* was found and depth-charged on 17 July, by a Whitley aircraft of No 502 Squadron in conjunction with a Lancaster of No 61 Squadron north-west of Cape Ortegal. The boat slid stern-first into the sea, and the entire 48-man crew perished.[7]

2 Convoy Attack!

17 TO 20 JULY

BY MIDDAY on 17 July 1942, as Bigalk's boat succumbed to airborne attack, *U 564* had reached the central Atlantic, the perils of Biscay finally left far behind. The boat had already travelled over 370 nautical miles surfaced, forced under for a further sixty by the increasingly effective Allied air patrols. Teddy had obtained confirmation from BdU concerning his request for refuelling from *Milchkuh*, and *U 564* droned steadily westward through a mild swell towards her rendezvous. Teddy correctly reasoned that, despite Gabler's ability to squeeze fuel into every spare centimetre of bunkerage, each drop of extra fuel that could be gathered now would allow a longer stay in the distant Caribbean arena of combat, where rich pickings were still on offer among Allied tanker and cargo traffic.

However, that night, as senior *Funkmaat* Rudi Elkerhausen monitored the constant flow of radio traffic generated by Dönitz's tight operational control of his 'Grey Wolves', news was received from flotilla-mate *U 202* of a potential diversion from their quiet ocean crossing: '2207hrs. KR KR. Convoy observed BD 6979. Course 250, speed moderate.'[1]

Kapitänleutnant Hans-Heinz Linder's boat was returning from a patrol of the United States' eastern seaboard, during which he had landed four saboteurs as part of Operation 'Pastorius', the first major sabotage mission in the United States to be planned by the Germans.[2] Bereft of torpedoes following a successful patrol, Linder shadowed the sighted merchant columns as contact boat, providing regular beacon signals and directional information for any U-boats within striking range. Even had he still carried torpedoes, Linder, as contact boat, would have been compelled to wait for other U-boats to reach the convoy before beginning any attack. Weighing his position against that of the convoy, Teddy reported to Dönitz: 'My location is CE 20. *U 564*.'

Hundreds of miles to the east, Dönitz's command staff, ensconced within their new headquarters in Paris on the Avenue Maréchal Maunoury, marked the newly reported contact on the enormous map that graced one entire wall of their operations room. On this complicated grid chart of the Atlantic Ocean were revealed the currently known whereabouts of every U-boat and the supposed locations for the elusive Allied targets. In his requisitioned château at Angers, closer to the Biscay ports, FdU West, Hans Rudolf Rösing, did likewise, his being the only true copy of the BdU situation chart.[3] Soon, encoded Morse instructions were echoing through the massive French transmitters under Rösing's care as Dönitz ordered in all boats within striking range for the kill. Aboard *U 564*, Elkerhausen handed his captain the hastily decoded message. 'Linder, hold contact with enemy, as long as fuel level permits. Suhren and *U 654* – get stuck in! [*Suhren u. – 654 ran!*]'

Although the reported sighting was some distance to the north-east, Teddy had already ordered *Stabsobersteuermann* Karl 'Stürkorl'

Work continues on the 8.8cm deck gun.

Limburg to plot an intercept course, confident that Dönitz would vector him into action. Alongside *U 654*, the *dreimal schwarze Kater* boat charged into pursuit at 15 knots, soon joined in the hunt by the large Type IX boat *U 108*. With constant position reports flowing from Linder, their chances of contact were considered good, and Teddy ordered all five electric torpedoes ('*Etos*') run out of their tubes and checked for any potential defects, re-greased and made ready for action. The *Etos*' eight-foot long batteries were checked and topped up with electrolyte by Ehlers' two torpedo crewmen, and a small series of heating elements within the battery container were switched on, pre-heating the cells before firing and thus extending the range of the torpedo by sixty per cent.

As Gabler's diesels roared into high revolutions, all unnecessary crew turned in, ordered by their captain to take the opportunity for rest while it presented itself. Teddy himself could not relax. He became a constant fixture atop the conning tower with his watch-keepers, anxiously sweeping the ocean for any signs of their quarry. Steaming cups of strong black coffee were relayed to the bridge from Hausruckinger's poky galley, and soon the unmistakable 'kick' of caffeine tightened the already anxious nerves of the lookouts.

Beyond the horizon, the thirty-five ships of convoy OS.34, en route from the United Kingdom for the stifling heat of Freetown, had become aware of their unwanted shadow. The OS (Outbound – South) route had been opened during 1941, ships bound for the South Atlantic, Panama and the Caribbean travelling under the protective umbrella of Western Approaches Command as far as Freetown, the inexorable southward expan-

With the hunt on for convoy OS.34, *U 654* rejoins Suhren's boat, IIIWO and *Stabsobersteuerman* Karl Limburg communicating with the comrade boat by semaphore, standing on the *'Wintergarten'* 's railing. His counterpart aboard *U 654* is just visible.

Even in a mild swell of only two metres, the bow of a Type VIIC would regularly cut under. Here, *Oberleutnant zur See* Ulf Lawaetz and his three men of the First Watch scour the seas for shipping. The heavy rain gear used by U-boat crew, nicknamed *'der Grosse Seehund'* (the Big Seal) was not issued to every man; rather, the crew shared the few sets carried aboard.

sion of U-boat warfare necessitating this detour. By July 1942 the Admiralty had lost only thirteen out of a total of 1,343 escorted OS merchant ships, three of them wrecked in the North Channel only a day from port. Smaller in size than the average convoy plying this route, OS.34 had been formed from ships sailing from the Mersey, Milford Haven, the Clyde, Belfast and Oban, each 'feeder convoy' under local escort by anti-submarine trawlers. Eventually, as the thirty-five merchant ships formed into nine orderly columns, the task of their protection was handed over to the ocean escort on 12 July – five sloops of the 15th Escort Group, all fitted with HF/DF equipment. HMS *Folkestone, Gorleston, Wellington, Orissa* and *Erne* shepherded their precious charges out into the North Atlantic battleground, all sensory equipment at high alert as well as crow's-nest lookouts on constant rotation.[4]

Aboard HMS *Folkestone*, the escort's senior officer co-ordinated the four sloops that accompanied his own as the compact mass of shipping sailed at eight knots on a broad front via the North Channel before beginning its southward turn towards West Africa. The escort commander's civilian counterpart, the Convoy Commodore, R. G. Clayton, travelled aboard the SS *Empire Stanley* at the front of the middle column of four ships. Despite the previous low casualty rate, the fear of a U-boat attack still permeated the rows of merchantmen as they formed up into their columns. The broad front and shallow depth of the convoy were felt to offer the best protection against U-

boat attacks on the vulnerable flanks, escort ships of Western Approaches Tactical Command roving the fringes in search of German predators.

As Linder's repetitive beacon flashed into the ether towards his approaching comrades, the transmissions were instantly picked up elsewhere within the United Kingdom. Although unable to read the coded German message, powerful direction finding antennae had triangulated and localised its source, and an ominous message was

Kaptitänleutnant Forster swings *U 654* around to approach Suhren's boat from the port bow. This time the two passed so close that the commanders could communicate by megaphone, or as it was known, the *'Geflüstertaschel'* (whisper bag). Forster's distinctive *Wappen* of the White Elephant's head is plainly visible painted on the front quarter of his conning tower.

transmitted in cipher from the Admiralty to the Royal Navy escorts: 'Immediate. D/F on 11,068 K/cs at 2009 suggests that OS34 has been reported by a U-boat.' As guns were closed up in preparation aboard the sloops that flanked OS.34, a further transmission added to the growing sense of approaching danger aboard the British ships: 'D/F . . . suggests probability that two further U-boats are in the neighbourhood of convoy.'

However, Linder's strong beacon signals allowed the sloops to run down their own 'huff-duff' contacts vectored on *U 202*'s transmissions and eventually succeeded in forcing him away from the convoy body. But the veteran U-boat skipper was not easily dissuaded, and he doggedly attempted to regain touch until the other hunters arrived. Throughout the night the deadly jockeying for position by U-boat and sloop kept Linder at bay, but it ultimately failed to safeguard the merchant train, the British being constantly aware of their shadower and his gathering comrades.

When dawn tinged the thickening cloud banks of the eastern horizon with colour, Teddy had at last turned into his bunk to recharge his own batteries. As the sun slowly arced overhead, weakly filtering through the overcast sky above an uncharacteristically calm sea, the tranquillity of the ocean immediately surrounding *U 564* seemed marred only by the sleek grey hull of the German war machine. *U 564* was primed and ready for action as she followed Linder's estimated position reports. Eventually, at 1150 hours, the lookouts' concentration was rewarded with the unmistakable smudge of merchant smoke off the port bow, soon followed by the matchstick masts and wallowing hulls of Allied freighters. With Teddy in firm contact and the other two boats fast approaching, Linder, low on fuel, broke off his pursuit and headed for home, escaping a final burst of long-distance gunfire from an escort as he let go of his quarry and retreated at full surfaced speed.

Aboard *U 564*, Teddy and his officers scanned the distant target and pondered their best approach. Within the hour the decision was made, and a brief smattering of Morse flashed from the U-boat's forward antennae before Teddy dived to begin an underwater assault, the boat's bow pointing directly ahead of the convoy's path.

Foiled in his initial submerged attack, Suhren begins the chase again. *U 564* thunders into the evening, all eyes intent on their quarry's distant smoke trail.

In far away Paris, Dönitz received Teddy's brief transmission as tension mounted among the assembled staff officers: 'Convoy Grid BD 9592, attacking. Suhren.' Teddy's updated position was added to the Atlantic grid chart, and the small track that represented OS.34 was also moved forward as Dönitz's staff, most of them first-hand veterans of the war at sea, waited for further news.

The familiar welcome mixture of apprehension and excitement gripped *U 564*'s entire crew as Gabler brought the boat to an even keel at fourteen metres. Teddy sat astride the small saddle of the attack periscope, ensconced within the conning tower. Raising the slim periscope until its head barely protruded above the surface he began to estimate the necessary ranging information for torpedo attack. Conditions were not ideal for a submerged attack, and even the barest trace of a periscope wake would alert the escorts roaming the flanks of their precious charges. Two corvettes led the convoy's tightly formed columns while the three others acted as sentries for the vulnerable edges. They had stayed at Action Stations since Linder's initial contact, and were only too well aware of the German menace stalking their every move.

Through the delicate cross-hairs, Teddy selected his targets for an initial torpedo salvo, quietly reciting information for *Bootsmann* Webendörfer at his torpedo computer action station, sharing the confined space of the tower with his captain. Suddenly, as the moment of attack edged nearer, OS.34 tacked away to starboard and beyond range, and so the dance between hunter and hunted began again. *U 564*'s periscope had been seen, as evidenced by the sloop HMS *Gorleston* charging briefly toward them, and Teddy discreetly went deep, showing the enemy his boat's stern.[5] Action Stations were cancelled aboard the U-boat, and once Teddy had returned to periscope depth and watched the convoy virtually disappear to a range of twenty nautical miles, *U 564* heaved free of the deep to restart its surface chase. This time, she was not alone.

Forster's *U 654* glided into view astern, and, as the boats drew parallel, the two commanders communicated by flag and megaphone, Teddy guiding Forster on to the target: 'C[aptain] to C[aptain], I am in contact with enemy. Steer same course as me and do not get closer to them.' 'Message received and understood.'[6]

Forster surged ahead to gain his own advantageous position along the convoy's track, and the two boats swiftly parted company. The decision to await nightfall had been agreed, and the Germans skirted their exposed prey at a distance considered safe from detection. *U 108* and a further Type IX, *U 126*, were also rapidly approaching, and Teddy felt able to loosen the reins on his target, several coal-burning steamers betraying OS.34's position as they trailed thick plumes of smoke, their sweating engineers frantically stoking aged engines to keep pace with the rest of the convoy. The poor quality of coal carried aboard the SS *Port Auckland* and SS *Port Adelaide* provided dense exhaust smoke and made trailing the convoy 'a simple operation'.[7]

By evening, Teddy was noting the unwelcome presence of an enemy aircraft overhead, a Coastal Command, No 120 Squadron Liberator emerging from the dusk to overfly OS.34 for nearly an hour. Although correctly convinced that the bomber had spotted him, Teddy suffered no harassment or attack, but constant crash-dives as the aircraft circled toward him began to frustrate Suhren:

LI, up to periscope depth—again. Up and down the whole time; it's like being in a lift! These fiendish air patrols of the Allies . . . Up above it is getting dark; night is beginning.

'First and Second Watch Officers to the Captain! Listen in; when we surface now, we'll split up the four sectors between us—and keep your eyes open. Wooden eye—stay alert!'[8]

The significance of the moment appeared to be lost on Teddy, but this was the first time that aircraft had penetrated so far into the Atlantic. The Liberator bomber had been stripped of much of its bomb load for the installation of extra fuel tanks, although its value as a reconnaissance tool still warranted its presence. Although later rated by the Royal Navy as of 'little value, as endurance only allowed a brief visit', the Liberator was a harbinger of grim tidings for the U-boat service because, with the unqualified success of long-distance aircraft in reconnaissance and attack operations, during spring 1943 enough of these VLR aircraft would be available to plug the 'Atlantic Air Gap' that had offered safe haven to U-boats on the surface. Within OS.34, uncertainty crystallised into deep anxiety when the Liberator flew overhead, signalling to the convoy below that two U-boats had been sighted ahead of the merchantmen's track.

Gradually the last vestiges of day disappeared beneath the funereal shroud of nightfall. A mild wind furrowed the sea into the barest swell as *U 564*'s crew once more went to Action Stations. The pressure of the chase had begun to affect everything, even the calm composure of Teddy himself:

I keep concentrating on the puffs of [coal-burning] smoke and warn the watch not to startle me by shouting. They are to point out any occurrences in good time—and quietly! My nerves aren't made of steel! I stay glued to the smoke cloud too and don't dare close my eyes for a moment. Suddenly I hear a lookout on my right say, discreetly, 'Plane!'[9]

Once more the watch tumbled through the conning tower to land with the crash of hobnailed sea boots on the Control Room decking,

The following day dawned with seas calmed once more. However, the elements could change within minutes, and lookouts prepared for the rain squalls and short, steep seas that soon followed. This is *U 564*'s second watch. In the foreground, left, is Heinz Schmutzler, with Ernst Schlittenhard beside him, peering through binoculars. In the right background is the IIWO, Herbert Waldschmidt, and Heinrich Bartels is standing with his back to the camera. The attack periscope is partly raised, affording a good view of the spiralling wires designed to reduce both vibration of the scope through water and the wake that it left behind.

pulled out of the way by helping hands to avoid the next man coming down. *U 564* tilted alarmingly as Teddy's crash-dive sent the boat plunging to the depths, propellers biting deeply into dense seawater.

But there was no attack, and no thundering aerial depth charges, and again the German crew considered that they had battled the odds and won, unaware that the aircraft possessed neither depth charges nor bombs. Gingerly, Gabler returned the boat to periscope depth and Teddy used the larger navigation periscope to scan the heavens in search for their would-be attacker. The Liberator had retreated and continued to circle the convoy for nearly an hour before slipping completely from view.

Bartels and Waldschmidt ceaselessly traverse the limits of their visible horizon. It was a wearying task for four hours at a time, but it marked not only the difference between success and failure in convoy acquisition but also that between life and death: at this stage in the war, lookouts were the only means by which potential threats could be identified.

At 0030 hours on 19 July, the third day of the pursuit, *U 564* emerged once more from the deep, diesels exploding into life as Teddy raced ahead of the convoy path. This time he would go in for the kill, his crew once again at Action Stations. Neither of the other two U-boats in contact had made their presence truly felt, and Teddy decided on the risky technique of lying dead ahead of OS.34 and allowing it to come to him before opening fire. After less than an hour of full speed, he was in position and the lead sweepers of the convoy escort, HMS *Gorleston* and *Orissa*, emerged from the gloom. They headed slowly for the surfaced *U 564*, her engines barely idling as Teddy positioned himself for the attack. Pointing northward, *U 564*'s slim silhouette was virtually invisible to the southbound Allies, the two leading sloops floating past on either flank, ignorant of the lurking ambush since they were unequipped with that vital tool, centimetric radar. The columns of merchant shipping ploughed towards him as Teddy allowed the convoy to draw alongside, and, opening the outer torpedo doors to all four bow tubes, Teddy prepared to fire, lying unseen between the outermost starboard column of shipping and the flanking warships.

(Left) *Bootsmaat* Heinrich Bartels scans the port bow quadrant of the watch. Each lookout was responsible for a 90-degree sector. While during dawn and dusk extra men were sometimes added to the watch to compensate for poor visibility, from late 1942 onwards a fifth crewman was on almost permanent watch to search the skies for aerial threats. The MG 34 machine gun, one of two carried by *U 564*, was for additional anti-aircraft defence, although it was of limited use.
(Below left) '1150 hours: BD9861—convoy sighted!' In calmer seas, Suhren and Gabler (foreground) study the distant ships of OS.34. IWO Lawaetz waits for his captain's decision regarding their approach, while lookouts continue the watch as the U-boat is

The U-boat's crew could plainly hear the distinctive cacophony of propellers and engine noises reverberating through the water as OS.34 enveloped their boat. At that point Teddy realised that he was actually too close to his targets, and he swung his boat to starboard before easing back 90 degrees to port and waiting until the ships steamed into his line of fire. Teddy gently nudged *U 564* into reverse, lest he be caught in the blaze of exploding torpedoes, before quietly instructing Lawaetz at the UZO which targets to take. The firing position was ideal, with overlapping ships passing slowly before the U-boat's tubes. Teddy chose three middle ships—a pair of estimated 5,000-ton freighters and a third passenger-freighter, guessed at 8,000 tons. The latter ship sported a high superstructure and two funnels, although the thought nagged at Teddy that the second funnel could perhaps be false—the sure mark of an armed merchant cruiser.

Finally, at 0230 hours, the moment of truth arrived: *'Rohre einer bis vier, Los!'* In the bow compartment, *Mechanikermaat* Ehlers hammered down on all four firing levers and the torpedoes were propelled from the tubes, engines igniting to begin their run to target. Within only twenty-two seconds, all four G7e 'eels' were out and running true, the clang of the heavy pistons forced back against the torpedo tube doors showing four perfect launches, and stopwatches soon began to count off the vital seconds to impact. The quartet of lethal tor- pedoes sped away from *U 564* towards their targets. The small DC electric motors had engaged the second that the 'eels' were pushed free of the boat by the burst of compressed air, the torpedoes surging ahead to their maximum speed of 30 knots as they streaked toward destruction only metres below the surface. Virtually no wake was visible to betray the deadly projectiles to watching Allied lookouts, and at such close range only seconds would pass before the U-boat crew would realise either the flush of victory or frustrating failure.

With no time to lose, Teddy barked urgently for the boat to be thrown hard to port so that he could begin to escape the cordon of escorts, simultaneously bringing tube number five to bear on the merchant ships. But before *U 564* had half-completed her turn—less than two minutes after firing—all hell broke loose within the convoy: 'Two flashes and billowing black clouds. After that a third ear-splitting bang, a massive burst of flame and an entire steamer flies into the air. It's the one with two funnels; it carried a load of munitions.'[10]

Confusion enveloped the scene as a fourth exploding torpedo was heard. The spectacular fireball that had once been the 5,724-ton SS *Empire Hawksbill* threw the panorama into stark relief as the German attackers stood awestruck before the dazzling orgy of destruction that they had unleashed. The South Western Shipbuilding Company, San Pedro, California had built the veteran steamer as SS *West Nivaria* for the US Shipping Board in 1920. She had undergone two name changes before being sold to Britain during its hour of crisis in 1940. Her new homeport designated as London, she had been converted to a DEMS (defensively armed merchant ship) with the addition of a 4-inch gun and scattered machine guns and renamed *Empire Hawksbill*.[11] However, after surviving two years of war service for Britain, neither she nor her master, Captain Harold Theodore Lamb, nor his crew of thirty-seven and nine gunners for the single deck cannon, stood a chance. The SS *Empire Hawksbill* was one of eight ships in the convoy carrying explosives, and, as the torpedo warhead rapped against her hull, the sympathetic detonation of stored ammunition bound ultimately for Table Bay, South Africa, ripped *Empire Hawksbill* and its human contingent to pieces, vaporised with their cargo.

Fragments rained down around *U 564*, and, fearing for their safety, Teddy ordered his watch below to shelter while he remained rooted to the spot by the pyrotechnic display. The bow of an escort ship slid between *U 564* and the blazing remains of the freighter, and Teddy jerked his eyes away, shouting for Haring to come to the bridge and record the moment with his camera. But suddenly a stunned Teddy heard the unmistakable hiss of air escaping from the U-boat's diving cells, and *U 564* began rapidly to nose-dive underwater.

> What the devil is going on? Bucketfuls of water are starting to crash on my head as I pull the hatch shut behind me . . . I'm furious.
>
> 'Have you all taken leave of your senses? Whose job is it to give the Alarm on board? Who gave this order?!'
>
> '[Stürkorl] is completely taken aback at being shouted at. 'But, Boss, you gave the order yourself'

'Who . . . what . . . how?' Heavens, what the poor chap has done is perfectly reasonable. When I send the bridge watch down, as I had done in this case because of all the debris raining down, it's always a prelude to an 'Alarm'.

But . . . I didn't shout alarm this time, but 'PK man' — in fact 'PK, PK'. Our bloody passenger from the Ministry of Propaganda![12]

For the next ten minutes Teddy was apoplectic with rage as he sent for the hapless Haring and vented his frustrations upon him within the crowded Control Room, using terms that were eloquently naval in origin. Gabler eventually interrupted the torrent of abuse by quietly announcing that the boat lay at 100 metres, the sound of approaching propellers heralding an inevitable counter-attack from above. At the hydrophone, *Funkmaat* Rudi Elkerhausen tracked the approaching threat and Teddy quickly ordered the newly installed 'Bold' ejector used, the fizzing sonar decoy launched from the stern compartment as *U 564* began evasive manoeuvring. This time she was lucky: the six depth charges launched by HMS *Gorleston* as part of the pattern attack against the presumed location of an enemy submarine, Operation 'Raspberry', detonated around the effervescent 'Bold' capsule, and *U 564* crept away to make good her initial escape.

The use of 'Bold' had aided underwater evasion enormously. Most experienced U-boat commanders would make every attempt at a surface run, where the U-boat's slim silhouette and good turn of speed could be fully used to advantage (during summer 1942 Allied surface radar was not yet in widespread use and was still unknown to the *Kriegsmarine*). However, if forced below, or, in Teddy's case, taken there by accident, the 'Bold' sonar decoy was almost always launched in an attempt to scramble any probing ASDIC from above.

The decoy pre-empted and closely matched an idea later spoken of in conference between Adolf Hitler and senior *Kriegsmarine* officers in Berlin during September. There, the *Führer* expressed a desire for a 'decoy torpedo' to simulate the destruction of a U-boat. His original opinion was that special torpedoes carrying oil and various items of wreckage could be carried and launched in the event of a prolonged hunt by enemy destroyers. However, the loss of an operational torpedo tube for the carrying of such a device was unacceptable to U-boat officers. In the meantime, the compromise solution had already been reached that resulted in probably the most effective of various German sonar counter-measures. Named 'Bold' (short for *Kobold*, meaning 'goblin'), this device comprised a 15cm diameter capsule filled with 370g of calcium and zinc compound packed within a wire mesh bag, in turn stored inside an aluminium canister. The canister was expelled from the U-boat's stern compartment through a purpose-built ejector (named the *Pillenwerfer* — pill-thrower — by crewmen). Sealed within its waterproof aluminium outer layer, a hydrostatic valve controlled a trickling entry of seawater into the canister, which was designed to remain at neutral buoyancy at a depth of around thirty metres. Upon contact with seawater, the chemical compound within produced hydrogen gas, resulting in a large mass of bubbles that, on ASDIC, resembled the echo produced by a submarine contact. A single 'Bold' capsule continued to emit bubbles for up to 25 minutes.[13]

As Teddy's men waited to see whether the 'Bold' decoy would indeed cover their retreat, above them OS.34 was re-forming after the devastating attack. Blinding starshell burst above the convoy, adding to the ghastly illumination provided by the burning remains of two ships and discharged white distress rockets. Teddy was certain that he had hit four separate ships, sinking two and damaging the others; even in later years, the crew remained adamant that they had hit all four ships during that confused night action. However, according to Allied records of the clash, although he was correct about the two lost during the torpedo attack, no subsequent damage to any other ship was noted by the Admiralty. As well as the

obliterated *Empire Hawksbill*, the 5,372-ton MV *Lavington Court* had also been hit.

Built by Belfast's renowned Harland & Wolff shipyard for the Court Line during 1940, this sturdy vessel had received a single crippling blow. As the exploding *Empire Hawksbill* riveted most of the convoy with its awesome spectacle, the Chief Engineer aboard the *Lavington Court* glimpsed the barely visible but chilling trail of a high-speed torpedo approaching his ship and shouted for the master, Captain J. W. Sutherland, to alter course. But it was too late. Oddly, there was no loud explosion, nor pillar of water, to mark the impact, and at first Sutherland believed that the ship astern of his, the SS *Tuscan Star*, had been hit. In fact, the torpedo had struck in the aft peak tank, which was filled with fresh water, and little effect was at first registered. But the ship's steering gear had been destroyed and the propeller blown off, causing the *Lavington Court* to career out of control to port across the convoy's path. The crew's accommodation had also been destroyed in the blast, along with six men at rest there. With no control of his vessel, Sutherland ordered her stopped and abandoned after a search for survivors had been carried out, although rescuers were unable to penetrate the twisted wreckage of the accommodation room. As the lifeboats pulled away from their stricken ship, the 'Grimsby' class sloop HMS *Wellington* hove into view and rescued Sutherland in order to ascertain exactly what had happened. With so few escorts guarding OS.34, the remaining survivors were left behind, *Wellington*'s captain returning later to retrieve them.

Immediately after their attack on OS.34, and once emotions had calmed following their unplanned crash-dive, there was absolute silence aboard *U 564* as the crewmen awaited further retaliation. The distant sound of depth charges could be heard on the convoy's other flank as HMS *Folkestone* engaged *U 654*, and a steady drip of water from condensation and wet leather jackets added an eerie ambience to the interminable wait. Propeller noise from HMS *Gorleston* continued to criss-cross the waters above, and, rather than lie sluggish and vulnerable to ASDIC and depth charges, Teddy opted for a high-speed dash for safety on the surface. Soon, compressed air hissed into the buoyancy tanks and the boat began to rise, all crewmen standing by in preparation for their bid for freedom. Lookouts clustered around the conning tower ladder, red glasses preparing their eyes for the darkness outside. Above them, Teddy waited at the hatch itself, and as soon as Gabler announced the bridge free of the water he undogged the heavy lugs and rushed outside, scanning quickly

(Above) Eventually the two boats were called off from the hunt, the rest of OS.34 escaping further attack. After a final megaphone exchange, the two boats adopted parallel but widely spaced travel lines, both heading for the 'Golden West'.

to the left and right as the blazing *Hawksbill* continued to cast an ethereal glow on the recent battlefield. *Gorleston* lay a matter of only 800 metres astern and *U 564* wallowed in the swell between the escorts and the fleeing convoy as Gabler's diesel crew noisily fired engines and the boat began to surge forward towards the sanctuary of darkness:[14]

> We knew it was going to be a risky escape, but we also knew that on the surface, at night, end-on to the enemy, we were virtually invisible and able to use our top speed. Gabler could work wonders with those diesels.[15]

Suddenly the British sloop sprang to life and took up the pursuit, firing starshell and high explosive at the twisting U-boat. ASDIC contact, at first thought to be debris and a dubious contact at best, had been made with Teddy's boat while *U 564* had been submerged, and *Gorleston* had edged nearer until visual contact was unexpectedly made with the surfaced U-boat. Teddy ordered electric motors run in tandem with the racing diesels, and his speed crept slowly upward to 17 knots as *U 564* began to draw away from the sloop, *Gorleston*'s own heavily fouled bottom deducting at least two knots from a top speed that could, in other circumstances, have matched that of the U-boat. HMS *Wellington*, fresh from attending to *Lavington Court*, had meanwhile also joined the chase, and both ships were able to keep *U 564* within visual range as they hammered forward in pursuit. *Gorleston* barely missed colliding with an unidentified merchant ship that appeared without warning from out of a brief rain squall, and guns aboard the sloop were trained towards it in case of hostile

In the hours after *U 564*'s successful attack on OS.34, the four empty bow torpedo tubes were reloaded. The first step in this difficult procedure was the removal of the false wooden decking to expose the first pair of reloads. Here (far left) *Mechanikerobergefreiter* Wilhelm Bigge crouches between the 1.5-ton 'eels', preparing the chains with which they would be hoisted into position.

(Left) *Mechanikermaat* Gerhard Ehlers and Bigge prepare the suspended steel girders prior to attachment to the torpedoes.

(Below left) Ehlers, Bigge and *Mechanikergefreiter* Horst Becker lower the strong supporting beam in order to attach a torpedo before beginning to hoist it with chain winches into position, where it can be greased and slid into the empty tubes. While Bigge attaches the strong, clamped bands to the first torpedo (right), off-duty diesel 'stoker' *Maschinenobergefreiter* Reinhold Abel reads in the top bunk. The lower bunks are visible folded out of the way, and it was with some joy that the 'Lords' of the forward torpedo room greeted the first two reloads—once the pair of torpedoes were off the floor the lower bunks could be used and the incredible discomfort of living with even less room than usual eased slightly.

action. It was later found to be the SS *Ettrick Bank,* straggling from the main convoy body.

Soaked by the uncomfortably close fall of shot and garishly exposed by swinging flares above, Teddy bellowed for more power, his IIWO, *LzS* Herbert Waldschmidt, ducking involuntarily as a starshell exploded overhead and sheepishly registering his captain's bemused grin at the reflex action. Teddy's gamble was paying off, and only minutes separated *U 564* from safety as she outpaced her pursuit, the British shells falling wildly and abruptly ceasing as their target edged into the shadows. However, fortune had never graced Teddy with an easy path in life, and it was not to allow him so simple an escape.

Just as the race appeared won, *U 564* vibrated loudly and began to slow. Thick black smoke billowed from both exhausts and curled out of the conning tower hatch, spreading over the water and obscuring the pursuing Royal Navy ships. Teddy was aghast as *Obermaschinist* Hermann Kräh's muffled voice came through the voice pipes: 'Boat unfit to dive. Starboard diesel out of action.' Fire appeared to have broken out in the engine room, and the entire interior was plunged into darkness as smoke smothered everything, with men barely able to breathe amid the choking fumes. Suhren glimpsed the rapidly approaching sloops through brief gaps in the dense smoke, and, as the solitary port engine spluttered and showed signs of also giving up, he and the remaining watchmen plunged into the cloying interior, slammed the hatch shut and ordered the boat taken down to 150 metres ('A+70')—fire or no fire—as a British searchlight flashed over his conning tower. Gasping for breath, engineers cut the port diesel and threw the electric motors into full ahead, *U 564*'s bow dipping under while '*Bold*' capsules were ejected once more from the stern. All available men raced blindly for the bow torpedo room to hasten the emergency dive, *U 564* dangerously exposed to attack as she clawed for the sanctuary of depth. Gabler, his eyes streaming and with a handkerchief pressed over his nose and mouth in an effort to breathe, struggled to maintain trim as the boat surged through the water:

> The boat manages to dive, and I can hear the electric engines starting up. But I can't believe my eyes. Standing in the central area, I can't see my hand in front of my face. Smoke everywhere; everyone is coughing and choking. Has the lighting failed? Why hasn't the emergency lighting come on? The darkness persists, and the boat dives down. Judging by the sounds, we must be about 50 to 60 metres down.
>
> The LI is trying to get the boat level, but, as he trims her, *U 564* goes up at the bows again. We can't go on like that, sagging at the stern, and in the end we get

going with a dive. The air is full of smoke, thick enough to cut with a knife. We press handkerchiefs over our noses and mouths, and some grab the emergency breathing apparatus. Whilst we are all at sixes and sevens, the patrolling escorts are closing in at top speed, with fire in their bellies.[16]

Overhead, HMS *Gorleston* and *Wellington* charged forward and prepared to attack. The British were unaware of the drama taking place aboard their enemy, but believed the U-boat to have been making heavy way in what had become a short, steep sea with brief squalls of rain — a perspective revealed in the Report of Proceedings later written about the action:

> [*Gorleston*'s] C.O. was confident he could follow by eye, and fire was checked in the hope that quarry would relax, thinking he had shaken off pursuit. Pom-Poms and .5" Brownings were, however, trained on the target in order to counter any offensive action. At 0122 that expected and welcome smoke started coming from the U-boat, and it increased in volume until at 0135 one could almost hear one engine fall over, and range, which was by then 2,400 yards, started tumbling down until at 0139 relative rate of advance indicated that U-boat was stopped and image was reported as diving.[17]

HMS *Wellington* hauled ahead of her companion ship and hurled ten shallow-set Mark VII depth charges around the escaping U-boat. Though *U 564* was severely rocked by the blasts, there was not even mild damage aboard as the U-boat had managed to dive below the explosions. A further ten charges from HMS *Gorleston*, set to 50 feet and 140 feet, detonated around the *'Bold'* decoy, again proving the worth of this device. Aboard the sloops an unidentified — then as well as now — 'heavy explosion' was heard, leading the British to

(Below left) Once the torpedoes have been prepared by the three-man torpedo crew, the boat's other 'Lords' assist with the task of man-handling the hefty weapons into place. In the left foreground is the boat's cook Hermann Hausruckinger, preparing to assist with hoisting the 'eel' into position.
(Below centre) As Hausruckinger helps pull the cumbersome weapon into position, a clue to the boat's general destination can be gleaned from the white tropical helmet wedged above the top bunk folded out of the way behind him.
(Below right) After all bunks were folded away and the torpedoes successfully positioned, the latter received a liberal coating of grease before being slid slowly by hand-wheel into the distant tubes. Of interest amongst the equipment strewn on the floor are two paddles for the boat's inflatable rubber dinghies, stored beneath the decking.
(Right) Chief Torpedo Mechanic, *Mechanikermaat* Gerhard Ehlers — the only non-commissioned officer to sleep outside of the NCOs' quarters, bedded in the forward torpedo room with his precious 'eels'.

believe that their charges had landed on target. With both ships carrying out one further attack apiece on what were considered doubtful ASDIC traces, there was not yet time for celebration aboard the sloops, but they later claimed 'probable' victory: 'Although it was not possible to attempt to obtain any evidence, U-boat's depth and movements were so well known that I find it difficult to imagine that he escaped destruction from such a heavy pattern.'[18]

However, the presumed demise of *U 564* was premature. Although she was unable to vent the thick smoke, the latter slowly began to settle within the confines of the narrow pressure hull, and the tension that had gripped the crew receded proportionately. The anxiety aboard *U 564* had no doubt been eased somewhat by 'Stürkorl' Limburg as he stood impassively at his navigation table. In his loud Thuringian voice, he calmly expressed the opinion to all within earshot that it was 'as dark as a bear's arse in here.'

Somewhat incredibly, they had escaped. The sloops' propellers slowly vanished into the distance. The fire had been brought under control at a depth of 120 metres after water had been deliberately leaked into the pressure hull to extinguish the blaze, CO_2 extinguishers having failed to smother the flames. Realising the narrow margin that had separated the boat's survival from sudden death in a deluge of depth charges, Teddy prudently waited underwater for the enemy's propellers to vanish completely from the hydrophones:

> I wipe the sweat from my brow and breathe again. They've gone . . . Gradually it gets lighter inside the boat. The bulbs of the emergency lighting glimmer through the smoke, which is slowly thinning. We turn and steer a westerly course, carefully keeping the boat level. Nothing more happens.[19]

Eventually, at 0545 hours, he ordered the boat surfaced, and *U 564* emerged to an empty horizon. Gasping lookouts crowded rapidly on to the bridge as fresh air flooded through the filthy interior. Everything was covered with a thick film of black soot, and Teddy ordered Gabler and Kräh, his Senior Diesel Technician, to the bridge to determine what had happened. Gabler had no answers as he had been pinned to his action station within the Control Room during the emergency dive, but Kräh managed to explain the unfortunate circumstances that had nearly led to disaster. Somebody—unnamed in both KTB reports and Suhren's autobiography—in the diesel crew had absent-mindedly left a small pile of oily rags balanced precariously on a ledge immediately above the diesel's exhaust pipe. With the frantic twisting of the boat during her high-speed flight, the rags had dropped on to the red-hot pipe and caught fire, falling from there into the bilge beyond anybody's reach. After eight days at sea, a considerable quantity of spilt diesel had accumulated within the bilge water, and this also had promptly caught fire. It was Kräh who had finally managed to crack open the exhaust vents and flood the bilges with seawater, putting an end to the oily blaze. In Teddy's words, it had 'small beginnings, but dramatic consequences.'[20]

As the crew set about the arduous task of cleaning almost every visible surface within the blackened U-boat, *U 564* again began to trail the last estimated direction that the convoy had taken. Torpedo tubes were reloaded and the boat was brought back to fighting trim. By 1400 hours *U 654* edged once more into view, Forster having been

Elsewhere, keeping *U 564* in peak fighting trim required constant ministrations from the boat's technical crew. While seamen aboard kept four-hour duty watches, the engineers maintained six-hour shifts. Here, as the boat moves underwater on electric motors, *Maschinenobergefreiter* Walter Labahn, a Port Diesel Stoker, works on changing a cylinder head of the engine under his responsibility.

The close confines of Labahn's working environment were difficult for Haring to capture on film since he was unable to shoot photographs from anywhere other than the narrow gangway that ran throughout the boat. Eventually, Labahn resorted to the time-honoured method of applied brute force, aided by the Diesel *Obermaschinist* Hermann Kräh, in his effort to loosen the holding nuts on the cylinder head so that it might be changed.

forced away from OS.34 before he could launch any attack. While *U 126* had failed to make contact, the third of the hunters engaged against the convoy, *U 108*, had also suffered dull fortune: each torpedo in a full salvo of six had missed its target before contact was lost. Teddy's victories remained OS.34's only casualties throughout the convoy's voyage to Sierra Leone.

U 564 and *U 654* hunted in company for traces of OS.34 throughout the day, and other boats, too, sought the elusive merchant ships. Suhren and Forster separated that evening as dusk settled over the expansive Atlantic. With the ferocity and anxiousness of combat now having passed, the crew unwound in whatever ways they could while bringing their boat back into shape. By the time night fell, there was

little trace of the blanketing soot from their minor blaze, and a brief commander's speech through the boat's tannoy system praised the crew for their coolness under fire, even the 'mutton head' that had left the oily rags unattended in the engine room. Despite recommendations from Kräh that the culprit be placed on a formal charge, Suhren demurred. He reasoned that it had not been deliberate but an act of absent-minded stupidity. The guilty man would have gone down with the rest of the crew if it had turned to tragedy, and the scowls he received from men scrubbing the blackened steel decking was punishment enough.

As *U 564* rolled through the darkness in mild Atlantic swells, Teddy called off the hunt, freed from the obligation by confirmation of his radio reports from BdU. OS.34 had escaped. The crew reverted to the tedious duty routine, stealing time within their bunks to read, carouse or sleep when off duty. For Suhren, as he sagged into his bunk with the familiar backache that plagued him during long periods of alert, the battle continued to play in his mind, the awesome spectacle repeating behind his closed eyes like a surreal movie:

> It had been a sight for the gods. Never again would I see the like of it at sea. The fireworks display of the blazing munitions ship was a unique experience. Pictures of that night etched themselves indelibly on my mind. The shadows of the escorts, the starshells above us . . .[21]

Now well aft of *U 564*, the badly damaged *Lavington Court* had, astonishingly, failed to sink, and her crew were later returned from HMS *Wellington* to inspect the damage. Four further injured survivors were also found still aboard, having climbed to safety from the porthole of the devastated crew's accommodation. Although she was deemed too dangerous to steam back to England and the crew had been disembarked, salvage was recommended, and two tugs under corvette escort were sent from Gibraltar in search of her. Finally, on 26 July, the tug *Prudent* found her. But, after securing strong towing hawsers to the deserted hulk and towing her for five days towards England, this valiant attempt at saving the crippled vessel failed when she foundered on 1 August.

The official report filed by escort corvette HMS *Rhododendron* tells of the ship's last moments:

> In position 49° 40'N, 18° 04'W steering 042°, 5 knots, *Lavington Court* suddenly disappeared. Have carried out A/S and starshell search with no result . . . do NOT [original emphasis] consider vessel was torpedoed. Consider vessel foundered through collapse of bulkhead . . .

Thus Teddy's second victim from OS.34 finally slipped beneath the waves days after the torpedo hit, taking 6,000 tons of military cargo, planned eventually for North Africa, to the seabed with her.

3 Survival, Rendezvous

21 JULY TO 1 AUGUST

THE BAPTISM of fire for *U 564*'s seventh war patrol had passed, claiming victory with no real damage to boat or crew. Despite losing all power in the middle of a high-speed chase and submerging with the U-boat's interior clouded with oily smoke, *U 564* had outwitted her enemies and lived to fight another day. To mark their deliverance, Teddy ordered the overworked cook Hausruckinger to prepare a 'celebration tea', the so-called *Geburtstagfeier* (birthday party). With an as yet ample supply of food from the carefully hoarded rations, Hausruckinger began to bake, and soon the boat's off-duty petty officers were enlisted to decorate the various creations with whipped cream and preserved fruit. The luxury of the moment was not lost on the weary crew, the officers wearing their best available attire as they prepared to enjoy Hausruckinger's handiwork.

Living conditions within the forward torpedo room had eased considerably since the brief convoy battle. With four torpedoes fired, the decking was now clear, as were all twelve bunks in use by the seamen housed there. However, the accommodation had already attained the characteristic unhealthy pall of U-boat life. Mildew had begun to affect the interior, a permanent sheen of humidity hanging in the air, clinging to clothing and unwashed bodies. This had caused yet another of the inherent problems of living in such conditions, one crewman in particular beginning to suffer the debilitating effect of confinement within *U 564*'s narrow steel tube. At 1736 hours on 20 July, Teddy radioed an emergency message to BdU command: 'We have a severe case of rheumatoid arthritis on board. Request transfer to returning boat at first possibility. Grid CF 7679. Suhren.'

It was *Matrosengefreiter* Ernst Schlittenhard who was suffering the agony of extreme rheumatism, his joints aflame with pain and his young body barely functional as he lay in his bunk stricken with the debilitating affliction. The Type VIIC, unlike larger Type IX and XIV U-boats, had no spare room to carry properly qualified medical personnel, and the Chief Radio Operator was customarily also the Medical Officer. Georg Seitz, *Oberfunkmaat* and thus medic aboard

U 604, another Type VIIC, explained the reasoning for this: 'We were the only members of the crew who could almost be guaranteed to have relatively clean hands. You can't operate Morse and write in the *Funk* log with oil all over your fingers.' [1]

But *U 564*'s designated medic, *Oberfunkmaat* Rudi Elkerhausen, possessed no more than the standard cursory first-aid knowledge, learnt at a brief course given for all such appointed medical personnel. Rheumatism was far beyond his ability to treat, and Teddy knew that Schlittenhard must be sent back to France in order to receive proper care. Unable to curtail his voyage, Teddy awaited instructions from Dönitz about how best to deal with the situation. With the constant shuttle of U-boats to and from France it would not be long before a suitable rendezvous could be arranged for the transfer of the unfortunate Schlittenhard to a homebound boat. As expected, a return message was soon received aboard *U 564* at a little past midnight: 'Mützelburg and Suhren to rendezvous in sector DG 4627, 23 July at 1000. Signal from Suhren in case meeting delayed until 1500. On completion, Mützelburg to send brief message "Ja"'.

Nearby, flotilla-mate *Kapitänleutnant* Rolf Mützelburg's *U 203* was returning home to Brest from a western Atlantic and Caribbean patrol that had seen five merchant ships sunk north and east of the Lesser Antilles. By meeting at the designated point, Mützelburg would be able to take Teddy's rheumatic crewman aboard and transport him to hospital in Brest.

Mützelburg was another of the 1st U-Flotilla's star performers, having carved a formidable reputation for himself in the Atlantic battle. The lessons that he had learnt as IWO aboard Joachim Schepke's *U 100* had been put to good use aboard his own *U 203*, and, with twenty-one confirmed sinkings, he had just received official acknowledgment of his award of the Knight's Cross with Oak Leaves by radio on 15 July. The perpetually cheerful Mützelburg and his expert crew would be in even higher spirits than normal when the two boats met to move Schlittenhard.

Indeed, it had become common knowledge that Mützelburg was one of Dönitz's four favourite officers, allowed to address their commander-in-chief using the familiar '*Du*' as opposed to more formal German '*Sie*'. Dönitz in turn called them '*Die vier Asse*' (The

Perhaps the most extraordinary pair of photographs taken of *U 564*'s engineering crewmen, these two photographs (below) show a man making an internal inspection of the port diving bunker. Neither the boat's log nor any surviving crew mention or remember the circumstances of this inspection, and it was highly unusual to make such an examination with the boat underway. Perhaps damage had been sustained during the depth-charging following the attack on OS.34 that required an immediate assessment to be made.

Regardless of war and its omnipresent danger, the presence of accompanying dolphins (right) holds a permanent and ageless attraction for seafarers.

Four Aces), Mützelburg, Erich Topp, Adalbert 'Adi' Schnee and Suhren constituting the privileged group. They were perhaps the leading lights of what was, in effect, the second generation of U-boat commanders. All had begun the war as watch officers, their erstwhile commanders now either dead, captured or ashore.

By the time the sun had risen, *U 564* was south-east of the Azores and heading south towards *U 203*, the island of San Miguel just invisible over the horizon. As the third watch of the day emerged into the light, clad in wet weather gear despite the clement conditions, the sleek grey hull of another submarine crept slowly towards them

on a converging course. It was the Type IXC *U 162* of the 2nd U-Flotilla. *Fregattenkapitän* Jürgen Wattenberg had departed Lorient on 7 July, bound for the Caribbean on the boat's second war patrol. The larger cousin of the small Type VIIC *U 564*, *U 162* was already a veteran of Caribbean operations, Wattenberg having sunk nine ships during his last foray to the coast of South America and the heavy merchant traffic off Guyana and Trinidad. After brief exchanges via megaphone and semaphore flag, the two U-boats separated once more and *U 564* continued towards her rendezvous with Mützelburg.

At dawn the following day, Teddy was woken with fresh coffee from a deep sleep within the tiny 'cabin' that marked the only personal domain of the captain. Crawling from his bunk, Suhren began to change out of his white cotton pyjamas ('one can only have a proper sleep in pyjamas, you know') when a more electrifying report was relayed from the watch on the bridge: 'Funnels to port!' 'I'm still in my pyjamas so throw a jacket over the top and go up on to the bridge. Yes, in fact two funnels!'[2]

Anxiously, Teddy and the lookouts scanned the distant contact with their heavy Zeiss binoculars, unable to identify their target. Curiously, the funnels did not appear to be moving in relation to *U 564*, which slowly skirted around them. The perplexing question of what they had blundered upon was finally revealed as the distinctive silhouettes of two Azores fishing boats emerged into plain sight, the sails taken for the smokestacks of larger ships. Shoulders slumped and the stress visibly relaxed, the news of their false alarm racing from man to man below

(Above) With over forty-five men confined into the narrow tube of a Type VIIC, a considerable amount of waste accumulated below decks. This was a problem made worse during enforced submersion, so commanders allowed the disposal overboard of as much as they could whenever possible. However, the issue of waste disposal was not always a simple one. Several accounts of merchant shipping being tracked by U-boat through its garbage trail exist, although the amount thrown overboard from *U 564* would probably pose no risk for the boat. Here (left) Ernst Schlittenhard maintains the watch while Heinz Schmutzler dumps the bucketful overboard.

After their narrow brush with disaster during the tussle over OS.34, Suhren ordered a 'celebration tea' (opposite). Off-duty *Funkmaat* Anderheyden was enlisted by the

overworked cook, Hausruckinger, to help decorate the cakes with whipped cream and preserved fruit. Anderheyden was soon joined in his labours by *ObMaschmt* Heinz Nordmann and Gerhard Ehlers (above right), although the photographic evidence of Ehlers' contribution remains doubtful — he appears to be more interested in verifying the worthiness of the whipped cream himself. Luxuries such as whipped cream were regularly carried aboard U-boats, usually in a locked food store and made available at the captain's discretion. Despite their often appalling living conditions, U-boat crews received some of the finest rations in the *Wehrmacht*.

decks. However, Teddy was still held by a vague sense of unease. His sixth sense told him that there was more to see, and he requested that his larger binoculars be brought to him on the bridge. Resting his elbows on the rim of the conning tower, he gazed once more at the two fishing boats. Suddenly, with an audible gasp, Suhren turned and bellowed for a crash-dive.

Directly behind the two fishermen emerged the clearly stepped outlines of two capital warships, a pair of British battleships escorted by a screening force of three destroyers. HMS *Nelson* and sister-ship HMS *Rodney* had been recently freed of their duty escorting convoy traffic bound for Freetown and were returning to Gibraltar. There they would join the massive build-up for Operation 'Pedestal' — the planned relief of the besieged island of Malta. The two imposing 'Nelson' class ships were easy to identify with their distinctive silhouette of three turrets mounted forward of the main superstructure. A formidable primary armament of nine 16-inch guns bristled from the main turrets, although from this considerable distance Teddy mistakenly believed that the *Rodney* sported only two turrets instead

The combined efforts of Hausruckinger and Anderheyden are greeted with due respect (top). The seat that Gabler and Suhren are sitting on within the Officers' Wardroom doubled as Gabler's sleeping place. Behind them can be seen latches for a proper fold-down bunk that was, however, in practice never used aboard *U 564*.

With all traces of the blanketing soot from their recent fire cleaned from the boat, the celebrations began in the Officers' Mess (above) . . . Suhren being responsible for the cake's even distribution. The IWO, *ObltzS* Ulf Lawaetz, awaits his piece with obvious anticipation.

Suhren, accompanied by Gabler, enters information into the boat's radio log book, or *Funkspruchkladde* (left). This was a written record of every message sent and received, and was the Senior Radioman's (Rudi Elkerhausen's) ultimate responsibility. The handwritten notations were later typed up and appended to the boat's War Diary (KTB) for BdU. In the background, *Bootsmaat* Heinz Webendörfer looks on, his hand resting on the UZO mounting. Within ten days at sea Ernst Schlittenhard had developed serious and debilitating rheumatism, requiring Suhren to radio BdU for assistance. Hours later, orders to rendezvous with *Kaptlt* Rolf Mützelburg's returned *U 203* and transfer Schlittenhard aboard were received.

of three. Impressive and valuable to the Royal Navy, the two battleships would have made a remarkable victory for *U 564,* and Suhren immediately prepared for a submerged attack as the British continued to head directly for him. With electric motors slow ahead, Teddy raised his scope to observe the impressive formation.

Anxiously, over the course of the next five hours, he waited to see whether he had been located, or whether the ships would continue their converging course and present him with near-perfect attacking conditions. As Lawaetz and Waldschmidt took their turns at the periscope to observe the enemy, it soon became apparent that *U 564* may indeed have been seen: the British ships swung westwards, still well out of range. Slowly they turned and began a sharpening tack northward at 15 knots, all the while over 8,000 metres away. With the U-boat's speed reduced by submergence, there was no chance of an underwater pursuit. There was little prospect of surfacing either: chasing the enemy on full diesel power was ruled out because of the fierce armament of the two battleships and their even more dangerous, nimble destroyer escort.

All Teddy could do was watch his enemy disappear from view, surfacing to an empty horizon and, less than an hour later, abandoning hope that the enemy would return. He contented himself with radioing news of the encounter and the enemy's projected course to BdU in anticipation that other German forces may find them. It was

a forlorn hope: none managed to make contact, and the two battle-ships safely reached their heavily protected anchorage beneath the shadow of the Rock of Gibraltar.

Early the next morning, Limburg's precise navigation brought *U 564* into grid DG 2633 in preparation for the rendezvous with Müt-zelburg. On cue, *U 203* soon coasted into sight as Waldschmidt and his three watch members climbed the tower to begin their stint on duty. As *U 203* approached from astern, Teddy ordered diesels throt-tled down to just above neutral, enough to keep steerage way on the grey steel hull. Easing into position to port of *U 564*, Mützelburg's crew broke out their small rubber dinghy, and shortly afterwards he and his chief engineer, *Oblt (Ing.)* Heinrich Heep, were aboard *U 564* and talking to Suhren and Gabler atop the conning tower.

Safe in the knowledge that they lay outside the range of Allied land-based aircraft, several off-duty seamen were granted per-mission to come above decks, and they clambered up the metal ladder to welcome the two visiting officers. The opportunity was taken by several of them to enjoy a brief swim in the sea, although it was still far from the tropical climate of their ultimate destin-ation. Meanwhile the virtually incapacitated Schlittenhard had been half-carried to the outer deck and aboard one of *U 564*'s own dinghies, along with his meagre possessions. While Webendörfer helped him into the small rubber boat, Heep ambled down on to the deck casing and jumped into the dinghy to return to *U 203*, taking whatever mail had already acc-umulated from Teddy's crew with him. Mützelburg, however, opted to swim, and, after briefly racing about the U-boat's deck with Her-mann Kräh and several of *U 564*'s own swimmers, he climbed

'24.7.42/0800. DG2633. U-boat in sight (Mützelburg).' During the morning of 23 July, as the first and second watches changed over *U 203* hove into view at the expected co-ordinates (below).

nimbly back once more on to the conning tower to perform one of his favourite tricks:

> They were playing tag when Mützelburg ran up the conning tower and dived in elegantly head-first off the top of the bridge into the water. My hair stood on end, and I said to him: 'What did you do that for? You wouldn't catch me doing that. It's reckless: the boat is so narrow that with its bulging fuel tanks on the side it's not that easy to dive across them.' But he laughed, and told me he did it quite often, and wouldn't be put off doing it. Then he continued on his way.[3]

After the successful rendezvous with Mützelburg's returning boat, Teddy continued the voyage towards his allocated combat zone. At that stage of the war, the U-boats considered themselves relatively safe within what had become known as the 'Atlantic Gap', where aircraft could not reach them, and *U 564* now travelled constantly surfaced until once again adopting caution when beginning to come within range of Caribbean-based aircraft. The boat made good time, each lookout watch succeeding the previous one with nothing to report during the crossing. Once again, Teddy capitalised on the absence of any aerial threat to permit his men some time above decks. Within the 'Gap', those crewmen off duty were allowed on to the conning tower to enjoy the sunshine, and Teddy also took the opportunity to shut down his boat's diesels and lie motionless in order that he and his crew could enjoy the luxury of outdoor washing and swimming:

> One place in the Atlantic between the Lesser Antilles and the European mainland was still not covered by aircraft, so I gave the crew permission to go for fifteen-minute swims—in sections, mind you, so that, just in case something happened, we could quickly submerge.[4]

Aside from whatever benefits such activities gave to morale, they also alleviated some of the distinctive health problems that sub-

There was, of course, a more practical reason for the two boats' rendezvous: *MatrGef* Ernst Schlittenhard's rheumatism had seen no improvement after he had spent all off-duty time within the dank U-boat interior. Transferred aboard the homebound *U 203*, he was returning to a Brest hospital. *Bootsmaat* Webendörfer helped the semi-invalid aboard the small dinghy, Heep making his own way on board before the two men were shuttled back to *U 203*, pulled from bow to stern to enable Schlittenhardt to disembark with greater ease.

In mid-Atlantic, east of the Colorado Bank, the two boats were safely within the 'Atlantic Air Gap' beyond the range of Allied aircraft and during the meeting several of Suhren's crew took the opportunity for a swimming break. Mützelburg afterwards made his own way back to *U 203*, swimming between the two boats after first diving headlong from *U 564*'s conning tower. As Suhren later remembered, 'My hair stood on end and I said to him, "What did you do that for? You wouldn't catch me doing that. It's reckless; the boat is so narrow that with its bulging fuel tanks on the side it's not that easy to dive across them." But he laughed and told me that he did it quite often and wouldn't be put off doing it.' In the photograph at bottom right, Mützelburg can just be seen making one last dive from his own boat before the latter's departure.

mariners faced. The dampness and humidity of the pressure hull had already claimed one man from Suhren's crew, and fresh sea air, water and sun eased cramped joints and helped keep many of the common skin ailments at bay. Once within the tropics, there would be myriad problems to face, the least of which were heat rashes that formed small white pustules beneath the skin. With the constant chafing of uniforms against them, these small boils would inevitably burst and cause considerable discomfort to the sufferer, as the raw flesh beneath rubbed against the fabric.

Once again, on 25 July, Forster's *U 654* slipped into view, mirroring *U 564*'s transit path. This time, with the two boats safely within the 'Atlantic Gap' there was the opportunity of a more social occasion between the two boats. Forster and his LI, *Oberleutnant (Ing.)* Bernard Klaasen, soon came aboard *U 564* to drink coffee in the tiny wardroom with Teddy and his off-duty officers. As well as coffee and biscuits, they also shared what-

Many crewmen from both boats were allowed above decks, clustered in their respective towers to wave farewell (left). The burst of steam and exhaust from *U 203*'s stern was created as the diesels were fired to begin their return to Brest carrying their sick passenger to hospital. Tragically, Suhren was to be proved correct when, seven weeks later, after *U 203* had left Brest for its eighth war patrol, *Kaptlt* Rolf Mützelburg called another swimming break in the mid-Atlantic for his crew. Diving again from the conning tower, he struck the boat's saddle tank as it rolled in a gentle swell and some hours later died from his injuries.

In preparation for receiving extra torpedoes from *U 154*, the opportunity was taken to download the externally stored 'eels' into the pressure hull (below). It was a time-consuming and laborious task, and the absence of enemy aircraft was a prerequisite for the safety of the boat. Helped by as many off-duty men as were available and could fit on the crowded forward deck, Bigge prepared the pulley that would be used to winch the heavy weapon from its canister below the wooden decking.

Watched from the tower by IIIWO Limburg and Teddy (below right), the winch is slowly turned to pull the torpedo free, the deck gun traversed to port out of the way of the slowly emerging torpedo's tailfins.

ever information and tactical theories the men had gleaned, before the two boats parted company once more at 2315 hours.

Forster was another veteran of the U-boat war, a graduate of the Officer's Crew of 1936. He had been IIWO on *U 29* when, on 28 September 1939, Adolf Hitler had personally decorated the entire crew with the first Iron Crosses won by the U-boat service following *U 29*'s destruction of the carrier HMS *Courageous*. He had a brief stint in command of the training boat *U 62*, and during November 1941 he had taken command of *U 654*. Thus far in his career as skipper he had achieved during his previous three Atlantic war patrols the confirmed sinking of four ships, his first victim, French corvette *Alysse*, having

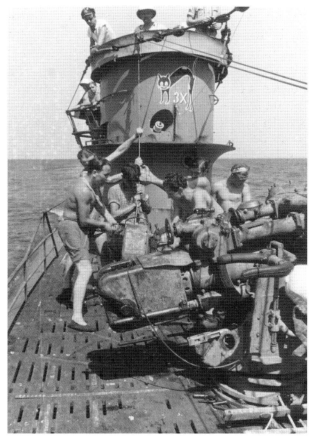

(Left) With willing hands helping as much as possible, Labahn takes his turn at the handle (far left). As the torpedo is lifted out of its canister and on to the prepared loading cradle, Gabler (in white helmet) oversees the operation. IIWO Waldschmidt stands further towards the bow.

Once removed, the torpedo was rested upon its cradle in preparation for being lowered inside the bow torpedo room (right). The now-empty canister was lowered by handwheel back into its horizontal position. When it was clear, the torpedo loading hatch was opened and the 'eel' was gently winched downward into the bow room (far right), where the heavy chain controlled girders eventually lowered it to the floor either for storage or reloading into the tubes. In the photograph below left, following the successful transfer, Haring shows the loading cradle in detail. The large ceramic insulators attached to the wires in the fore-ground reduced the risk of static electricity discharging from the U-boat's jumper wires. The wires themselves doubled as radio antennae, attached to the wireless transmitter via the thin electric cable visible only just visible connecting at the foremost insulator. The bow jumper wires were used for trans-mission and the stern wires for reception.

Following their arduous torpedo loading, free from any aerial threats and with a clear distant horizon, Suhren ordered engines stopped and allowed his men to take a swimming break (far right). Aside from the recreational aspect, there were also distinct advantages to this practice in terms of health as it brought men into the fresh air for both washing and the benefits of the sun's rays. Sores and boils were commonplace among U-boat crews bound for tropical waters and unable to leave the mildewed, humid confines of the pressure hull.

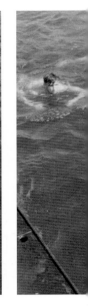

Diving from the bow of *U 564*, Gabler (top left, in the foreground) is dressed in attire known in German naval terminology as a 'peeled banana'. Even Suhren (above and left) took a dip in the warm Atlantic —one of the rare occasions when he divested himself of his red scarf. The *Kriegsmarine* also developed salt-water soap (below left), used by Teddy and his crew as Weben-dörfer sprays them with water piped from the engine room. Opinion remains divided over the merits of this soap: Suhren thought it wonderful; others were less than enthusiastic about the waxy residue that it sometimes left on the skin. Even in the midst of war there is peace (far left), as Suhren takes a moment to soak up the sun. (Right) On 25 July, Forster's *U 654* once more hove into view. This time, as the two boats met within the 'Atlantic Air Gap', Forster (left) and his LI, *Oberleutnant* (*Ing.*) Bernard Klaasen (right, in checked shirt), came aboard *U 564* for coffee and biscuits in the tiny wardroom with Suhren and his off-duty officers. Items like the fragile porcelain coffee pot were constant casualties of war, among the first things to break during a depth-charge attack or in particularly heavy weather.

been torpedoed on 9 February 1942. Unbeknown to any of the men gathered within that small panelled wardroom, a little over one month later Forster and his forty-three men would be dead, bombed into oblivion by a USAAF B-18 north of Panama.

On 30 July Teddy received notification of the proposed area for resupply of his boat from Leo Wolfbauer's *U 463 Milchkuh* U-tanker. The locale named by BdU was within the 36 square miles of grid square DD 9455 to the south-west of his present position. Course was laid, and *U 564* made good speed toward the rendezvous.

Combined with the fuel issue, another aggravation for Teddy was the loss of four of his precious torpedoes while en route for his final destination. Although they were put to valuable use, the thought of a reduced armoury within what promised to be a fruitful hunting ground gnawed at him constantly. As he pondered his quandary, inside the small Radio Room the rotating shifts of *Funker* decoded all U-boat signals traffic that clouded the ether between Paris and the Atlantic. Among them were several reports of boats returning to base, their torpedoes unspent and useless. With this in mind, and time to spare before the planned meeting with Wolfbauer, Suhren called together Gabler and Ehlers to put forward an unusual suggestion.

floating away in any current. As Haring balanced precariously on the periscope housing to record the manoeuvre, Gabler gingerly leaked air from the stern trim tanks and allowed the aft deck to become gradually awash.

As the stern disappeared altogether, calculations regarding the ability of the lifejackets to hold the weight of the torpedo proved correct, men swimming and using the dinghy were able to guide the cumbersome payload towards the bow where it would be positioned above a re-rigged cradle and allowed to float into place before tanks were blown with compressed air and U 564 was brought fully to the surface. Lifejackets were removed during the gradual rise of the U-boat, and the torpedo would then be ready for loading into the bow room.

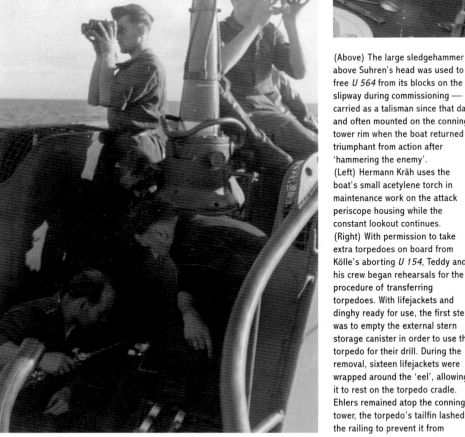

(Above) The large sledgehammer above Suhren's head was used to free *U 564* from its blocks on the slipway during commissioning — carried as a talisman since that day and often mounted on the conning tower rim when the boat returned triumphant from action after 'hammering the enemy'.

(Left) Hermann Kräh uses the boat's small acetylene torch in maintenance work on the attack periscope housing while the constant lookout continues.

(Right) With permission to take extra torpedoes on board from Kölle's aborting *U 154*, Teddy and his crew began rehearsals for the procedure of transferring torpedoes. With lifejackets and dinghy ready for use, the first step was to empty the external stern storage canister in order to use the torpedo for their drill. During the removal, sixteen lifejackets were wrapped around the 'eel', allowing it to rest on the torpedo cradle. Ehlers remained atop the conning tower, the torpedo's tailfin lashed to the railing to prevent it from

With cradles stowed once more, Teddy is captured by Haring's camera, triumphant but plainly tired from the exertion of their difficult transfer practice. The extended periscope is the navigation, or air search, 'scope, with the thicker shaft and larger head of the two. The navigation periscope was operated from the boat's Control Room, and, contrary to popular belief, while not generally used during submerged attacks, it was occasionally employed at night because of the increased light that entered the large lens. With no helicoil wires around it, the large shaft would leave more wake to betray the boat's presence during attack, and thus it could only be used safely in times of poor visibility.

Awaiting the arrival of *U 463*, lookouts broke out the tropical helmets as the equatorial heat increased. Beneath the front paws of the 'Three Black Cats' emblem can be seen the insulator through which the thin radio aerial entered the boat's pressure hull, running straight down the internal front of the tower and into the radio cabin.

U 564 did not possess the heavy lifting gear used to transfer torpedoes from one U-boat to another, but a small degree of ingenuity could allow the boat to take on 'eels' from one of their aborting comrades. Testing his theory, under the watchful eye of the boat's officers, the torpedo stored within the external stern container was lifted from its tube by eight of the crew using the boat's reloading tackle. Once free, sixteen lifejackets were wrapped around the 1.5-ton cylinder, its tailfin tied by rope to the *'Wintergarten'* in preparation for the next phase of Teddy's plan. With Ehlers grasping the fastened rope atop the conning tower, two rubber dinghies were inflated and the rest of the men held onto the torpedo as Gabler gently lowered the boat's stern until the torpedo, men and dinghies floated free. Ehlers ensured that they would not lose control of the precious weapon as men both in the dinghies and swimming alongside pushed the unusual load towards the boat's bow. There the 'eel' was man-oeuvred over the re-rigged and waiting bow loading cradle and the boat's semi-flooded tanks slowly blown clear by compressed air, bringing *U 564* up under the torpedo that the seamen nudged gently into place. Once fully surfaced the block and tackle were reattached to take the strain of the heavy torpedo, raising it free of the hatch which was opened and the 'eel' slid into place within the bow torpedo room. In a stroke, the problem of resupplying torpedoes at sea had been solved in little over three hours.

4 The U-Tanker

1 TO 11 AUGUST

ATER that day, final instructions for the meeting with *U 463* were received, and Teddy headed directly for the rendezvous. The message transmitted from Dönitz was exact, reflecting the tight control exercised by BdU:

At 1110 hours the first U-boat sighted was *U 654*, Forster arriving to take his turn at the same tanker rendezvous (right and below right). As Waldschmidt handled the watch, brief signals were exchanged by Limburg with Forster's boat.

1/8/42: 0055 2154

1. Begin an ordered supply from Wolfbauer from 1400 hours on 3 August. No radio beacon. Waiting boats to remain nearby in a cordon within signalling positions. Sharpest lookout. Caution against enemy submarines.

2. No unnecessary radio traffic, only boats arriving later than 6 August can make expected arrival reports.

3. Boats to take on: Senkel [*U 658*] and Holtorf [*U 598*] 68m³, Zurmühlen [*U 600*], *U 654* 60m³, Suhren 50m³, Neitzel 80m³, *U 129* minimum for return journey.

4. Finally, boats that have been done put 200 nautical miles between yourself and the tanker to allow continued refuelling of unreplenished boats.

5. Wolfbauer, after transfers, remain within 150 nautical miles of the area.

Two days later, Limburg's lookouts spotted the low silhouette of the first of the other U-boats gathering for refuelling, Forster's familiar *U 654* being followed thirty minutes later, at 1140 hours, by Witt's Type IXC *U 129*. Two hours on, the squat shape of *U 463* also came into view. *KK* Leo Wolfbauer was not untypical of many men who captained the large unwieldy tankers. At forty-seven years of age, he was considered far too old to hold command of a front-line combat boat. A veteran of the First World War, when he had served as watch officer aboard *U 29*, Wolfbauer had returned to active service during February 1942 to take command of *U 463* after a period as staff officer within the 24th U-Training Flotilla. With virtually no combat capability beyond air defence, the large tankers required a mature hand at the helm, younger officers being better suited to the rigours of the smaller hunting U-boats. This was the inaugural voyage for *U 463*, the hefty boat travelling directly for the Atlantic from Kiel.

The Type XIV had germinated from the seed of an idea put forward by Dönitz as early as 8 September 1939, when he had realised that the distances likely to be traversed in the coming war would require some form of ability to refuel at sea. Shorter, wider and deeper than

all other contemporary U-boat designs, the first Type XIV, *U 459*, sailed into operational use during May 1942, immediately proving its worth. The broad, flat upper deck provided ample room for the tanker's crew to manhandle supplies and fuel lines, though considerably inhibited the boat's diving time. Extra deck hatches had been provided to move stores from the interior for transfer to a waiting U-boat, but they were seldom used, the low freeboard being prone to swamping through openings much as aboard a Type VIIC. The Type XIV could carry 720 tons of extra diesel fuel, 34 tons of lubricating oil, 10.5 tons of fresh water and three tons of distilled.

As well as torpedoes, fuel and water, the U-tankers sported other useful capabilities, such as a small machine shop for repairs, numerous and varied replacement parts for combat boats, extensive

refrigeration units for fresh food and an on-board bakery capable of producing eighty 1-kilo rye-bread loaves every ten hours. Moreover, aboard *U 463* was *Marineoberassistenzarzt* Dr Fritz Walter Hoch, available for all who required medical treatment. In the case of *U 564*, it was an opportunity to transfer the boat's Control Room Mate, *Maschinenmaat* Emil Grade, aboard the large tanker for attention by Hoch. Grade had suffered what appear to be bloody and moderately severe head injuries. Curiously, no survivors that this author has spoken with can remember the event that led to Grade's injury, and it received no mention within *U 564*'s official log book. Indeed, even the log kept by *U 463* makes only passing

Within the hour, two more boats had arrived, Hans-Ludwig Witt's Type IXC *U 129* and Leo Wolfbauer's tanker *U 463*. Witt was scheduled to refuel first, taking the barest minimum required for a safe return to Lorient and the 2nd U-Flotilla base. Witt had had a successful patrol into the Gulf of Mexico, sinking eleven ships. The photograph at left shows *U 129* trailing astern of *U 463* to begin refuelling and taking aboard fresh provisions.

The large U-tanker's hefty free-board can be clearly seen as Wolf-bauer continues to transfer diesel to *U 129* (main illustration and right).

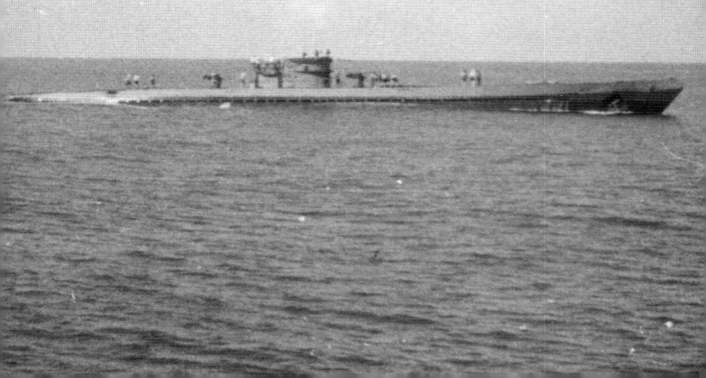

reference to the matter: 'Masch.Maat Grade from *U 564*, who has a head injury, taken on board.' As there is no further reference to Grade's return to *U 564*, and since he features in no subsequent photographs, one can only surmise that the wounds, possibly suffered during a hurried crash-dive, were treated as best as they could be at sea and that the patient returned to France with the tanker. The omission of this from Suhren's log book, however, is perplexing, as Schlittenhard's departure from the boat was clearly noted. It is possible that Grade was returned to *U 564*, although the apparent severity of the injury would make this unlikely.

It was Witt's *U 129* that first began the arduous task of taking diesel from Wolfbauer, and the two boats duly connected the heavy transfer hose, alongside which ran a telephone cable so that refuelling progress and resupply needs could be discussed. As they linked

At 1900 hours Suhren was able to begin his own refuelling, *U 129* having finished and sailing east for Lorient. The heavy fuel transfer hose and its guide rope was trailed behind *U 564* and hauled aboard by hand. Initially it appeared that the transfer was going to be problematic, the hose sinking without the required amount of flotation, but quick thinking and a short dip into the sea soon retrieved the recalcitrant hose.

together at 1420 hours, a fourth U-boat in need of fuel arrived — Karl Neitzel's *U 510*.

With such a conglomeration of surfaced boats, the need for strict and effective lookouts once more became paramount. Any unexpected arrival on the horizon would place them in extreme jeopardy, although at least in the summer of 1942 they were free from air attack within the region. With the 'Triton' 'Enigma' blackout in Britain, the steady stream of instructions for refuelling rendezvous were for the time being safe from prying eyes, although ultimately they would spell doom for the majority of *Milchkühe* during 1943. With *U 129* and *U 463* engaged on the pumping of fuel and dinghy exchanges of provisions and water, the remaining boats sailed at pace with them, forming a protective cordon around the centrally positioned tanker.

Finally, at 1900 hours, Teddy began his own refuelling. Initially it appeared that the transfer was going to be problematic as the thick heavy fuel hose trailing from *U 463* began to sink, lacking the required amount of flotation to keep it buoyant. The hose was normally inflated with air by a compressor (that was also used to flush the hose fully after use) as it trailed behind *U 463*, thereby providing the required buoyancy to allow the hose to be recovered. In this instance it had not been sufficiently inflated, although quick thinking and a short dip into the sea soon retrieved it. After securing the hose aboard *U 564*, men clustered on the bow to pull enough of the heavy tube across to enable it to be placed securely in position. Franz Stocker unscrewed the metal filler caps that led into the cavernous bunkers below, and the fuel transfer began. The two U-boats were connected for three and a half

hours, diesel pouring into *U 564*'s bunkers and fresh food and water being laboriously shuttled over by dinghy. The opportunity was also taken to carry further mail from Teddy's crew for the tanker, which would eventually take it back to France.

In fact, Teddy had already made suggestions regarding a more suitable fuelling hose that could be carried aboard *Milchkühe* as a result of a diesel transfer during his previous patrol into the Atlantic:

> Because the Type VII boats only take on diesel (30–40 cbm) and no lubricating oil, it is suggested that the tanker be given a light hose connector on board for this purpose, since the equipment available, with its heavy lugging cable and double hose lines, are altogether too heavy for the small amounts transferred. A French fire-hose (of sailcloth, strongly rubber-coated inside, 18.2 cm in diameter: rubber has been proved not to get eaten away) fixed to a manila rope has proved successful before now in transferring diesel to *U 107*. Tanker and boat could then, with this equipment and without any special lugging cable, travel in formation at 50m diagonally and about 50–100m abeam. The increased pumping time would then appear to be more than compensated for by the reduction in time spent setting up and dismantling, as well as the quicker flushing-through and blowing-out.

Franz Stocker helps Hermann Kräh guide the fuel hose into the filler tube (above). Signals between the two boats were facilitated by time-honoured semaphore, by mega-phone or by using a telephone line that ran alongside the hose. With virtually no way on the boat, the transfer of stores continued by rubber dinghy (right). As well as fresh bread and refrigerated produce, the bulky tin containers carried between twenty and thirty smaller cans of provisions, each dinghy in turn capable of carrying ten containers. Other large metal cans were used for the transfer of fresh water from storage tanks within *U 463*. IIIWO
(Far right) Limburg (front left) maintains the watch, megaphone at close hand should it be needed to warn men on deck.

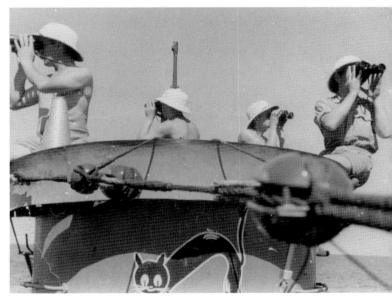

The main advantage would be that oil could be transferred in a bigger sea than up to now.[1]

While *U 564* refuelled, further instructions had arrived aboard the boat, this time concerning Suhren's request for fresh torpedoes. Although *U 463* carried enough extra fuel and supplies for several U-boats, she held only four extra torpedoes, all of which had been issued, so an alternative source had been found to replace Teddy's expended ammunition. Dönitz, although preoccupied with a burgeoning battle west of Newfoundland, where Karl Thurmann's *U 553* had managed to latch on to convoy ON.115, ordered Suhren to meet with *Korvettenkapitän* Walther Kölle's Type IXC *U 154* in grid square DP1455 to take over whatever ammunition he could, before carrying on to patrol the sectors EE and EO off the coast of British Guiana.

Kölle, a former company chief at Mürwik's naval school, had sailed from Lorient on 4 June, making the increasingly perilous Biscay crossing without serious incident before pounding across the Atlantic and entering the Caribbean Sea through the Windward Passage during early July. On 6 July, as *U 154* slipped through the Canal de Yucatán into the Gulf of Mexico, Kölle sank his first ship, the 65-ton Panamanian motor trawler *Lalita*, hammered beneath the waves with gunfire. It was to be Kölle's sole success.

During the next two weeks *U 154* patrolled the coasts of Alabama and Florida in search of targets, reporting two misses against a fast

The *Milchkuh* tankers also carried medical personnel; *Marineoberassistenzarzt* Dr Fritz Walter Hoch was aboard *U 463*. This remarkable pair of photographs shows *U 564*'s Control Room Mate, *Maschinenmaat* Emil Grade, being transferred by dinghy to *U 463* for treatment of a head injury. Oddly, Teddy's log book makes no mention of how he sustained the injury or of Grade's apparent transfer for a return to France. Crew chief Webendörfer supervised Grade's transfer, the injured man taking his sparse belongings (wrapped in the *Kriegsmarine*'s regulation checked sheet) and mail with him to the tanker.

enemy freighter near the scattered islands that comprised the Dry Tortugas. Otherwise, apart from neutrals, Kölle sighted no traffic, and he requested permission to proceed to Galveston in search of the elusive oil tankers known to be plying the busy Gulf of Mexico. To make matters worse for Kölle, U 154 was also hounded by an almost constant aircraft presence, local American defensive efforts having markedly improved since the beginning of hostilities within the region. Morale slumped as the boat prowled in sweltering tropical heat, the blight of tropical skin rashes and boils becoming commonplace among the men aboard as, because of the constant fear of aircraft, there was little chance for those not allocated lookout duties to go on deck into the sunshine and fresh air.

The miserable voyage was mercifully curtailed on 19 July when Kölle reported to BdU a leak in one of his fuel tanks, which was leaving a shimmering track of oil in U 154's wake. Unable to remedy the problem, Kölle appealed for permission to return to Lorient. After initially refusing acquiescence to shorten the patrol, Dönitz soon relented when Kölle began to also complain of feeling physically unwell. Eventually U 154 aborted her voyage and made way for Lorient, ordered to rendezvous with Reinhard Suhren's U 564 on 5 August.

Meanwhile U 564 had completed her refuelling, 50 tons of extra diesel resting securely within the bulging saddle tanks. Limburg laid in a new course for the next resupply meeting with the homebound Kölle, and U 564 swung away from the continuing refuelling of Forster's boat. Teddy's patrol to

Once the diesel transfer was complete, *U 463* dropped astern of *U 564*, supplies still shuttling between the two boats in dinghies hauled between them using ropes. Within three and a half hours the rendezvous was complete, and *U 564* laid course for her next meeting.

the Caribbean benefited enormously from the provision of a dedicated tanker within the mid-Atlantic, and, in all, thirteen U-boats would be supplied to some degree during Wolfbauer's maiden voyage, after which *U 463* sailed for St-Nazaire as a part of the 10th U-Flotilla.[2]

As *U 564* and *U 154* converged for their own private resupply, lookouts, now clad in only their shorts and occasionally the cumbersome white tropical helmets, ceaselessly scanned the distant horizons. Haring had become a familiar presence atop the conning tower, endlessly shooting newsreel and still photographs for his propaganda assignment. On 5 August, as *U 564* entered grid DP1455, the torpedo-loading cradle was assembled as Teddy began to hover within the prescribed area to await the arrival of Kölle's Type IXC.

It was Waldschmidt's watch that first spotted the distant matchstick masts of a ship over the horizon. Immediately the U-boat was put to Action Stations, Teddy diving to prepare for an underwater attack. As the approaching diesel-powered ship grew within his periscope, the name and nationality could soon be plainly seen: she was a neutral, the Swedish MV *Scania*. Built in 1934 by the Malmö yards of the Kockmus Mekaniska Verkstad company, the 1,629-ton vessel plied the American trade routes for the Rederi-A/B Svenska Lloyd shipping line, based in Gothenburg, Sweden.

Maschinenobermaat Heinz Nordmann (far left), in charge of the
port electric motor, relaxes atop the
conning tower. Nordmann had
served aboard U 564 since the
boat's commissioning and was an
integral and popular member of the
crew.
Oberfunkmaat Willi Anderheyden,
pictured at the same time (centre).
As Second Radio Petty Officer,
Anderheyden managed one of the
two watches within the radio and
listening room.
PK Maat Haring (left), photographed by Nordmann as U 564
travelled to meet Kölle.

Despite her neutral credentials, she was potentially within the prescribed blockade zone, and Teddy ordered U 564 surfaced and put into interception, the gun crew clattering up the small conning-tower ladder to take their positions at the 8.8cm as diesels thundered to push the boat forward towards her quarry. Webendörfer climbed down from the bridge to take immediate charge of the main gun crew, while the 2cm flak weapon was also manned and made ready to fire. All those atop the conning tower wadded cotton wool into their ears to protect their hearing from the sharp concussion of the 2cm fire—almost certainly the only weapon ready to use in order to bring the quarry to a halt. Ironically, the Germans' preparedness had worked against them. Although the main artillery crew, in their thick canvas harnesses and clutching numerous ready-rounds of ammunition, were an imposing sight through binoculars aboard the merchantman's bridge, they could not fire their weapon. The torpedo-loading cradle was directly beneath the cannon's muzzle as U 564 charged forward to intercept, vulnerable to the blast effects of such close-quarter artillery and liable to fracture.

Aboard the Swede there was, no doubt, considerable consternation. The manned and ready artillery piece added to the menace of an unheralded torpedo attack. Through high-power binoculars, several crewmen aboard U 564's conning tower could be seen cradling MP 40 sub-machine guns preparatory to boarding their freighter. The officers and twenty-five-man crew of the Scania, commanded by Captain Carl Isak Jansson, had already experienced the Atlantic war at first hand. Earlier that year, on 19 January, the Swedish ship had rendered fire-fighting assistance to American steamer SS Malay, alight and burning following attack by Kaptlt Reinhard Hardegen's U 123 engaged on Operation 'Paukenschlag'. The raging fires started by Hardegen's artillery were brought under control, and the American crew managed once more to get under way towards their destination—Port Arthur, Texas—despite a further torpedo hit from Hardegen, who had returned to the scene. Months later, on 12 April, the Scania again played the role of rescuer, picking up twenty-seven survivors from the Norwegian freighter MV Balkis, torpedoed, shelled and sunk off the coast of Brazil by the Italian submarine Pietro Calvi.

Aboard U 564, Waldschmidt steadied himself on the narrow ledge that bordered the conning tower and, using the boat's lamp, proceeded to signal to the distant freighter. His words, dictated by Teddy, flashed in international Morse code as the German submarine rapidly gained ground on its target. A swift burst of fire from the 2cm flak gun served to punctuate the order to stop and show the ship's papers, and soon the large ship was forced to comply, the screws powered by 7-cylinder MAN diesels slowing their steady beat and the way on *Scania* perceptibly dropping as, in the distance, men could be seen to approach a lifeboat. Waldschmidt's signal lamp ordered the Swedish captain to present his ship's log and manifest, and a small party of men, led by an immaculately uniformed merchant officer, were soon on their way towards *U 564* as the U-boat overtook her victim and circled around her now stationary bow.

The Swedish first officer, 32-year-old Stig Anders August Lundh, who doubled as the telegraph operator, was soon alongside, passing the required documents up to willing German hands before also climbing aboard. He was taken to the bridge and was soon face to face with Teddy, who began to study the *Scania*'s documents. Fortunately, Copenhagen-born Lawaetz, now wearing his peaked officer's cap, was able to converse with Lundh, and the neutral's course and destination were soon swiftly confirmed. *Scania* was heading, fully loaded, from Bermuda (originally New York) to Buenos Aires, and, unsure of the virtues of sinking the ship, Teddy contented himself with a warning to Lundh that the ship should make no use of its radio and must continue on its direct course out of the combat zone. With the most serious pose he could muster, he also declared that, should they meet again so near to the United States, he would probably open fire:

> So, because neutrals were not even safe so close to the United States, the first officer was very grateful that we were letting them go. Later, after he had returned he sent over breakfast for us, with fresh bread and so on. And also, the American food . . . well, it was different from what we could get in Germany: they didn't eat like us, and we enjoyed it! We felt that we had never eaten so well.[3]

After the brief but eventful interruption to its journey, the *Scania* departed and gradually disappeared from view. Although nobody could know it at the time, she would have one more fateful encounter with Dönitz's men. On 13 December 1942 the 10th U-Flotilla's *U 176* intercepted her as she sailed from Montevideo laden with goods bound for Philadelphia. Again, First Officer Lundh boarded the ship's wooden dory and went aboard the U-boat. There he produced the ship's manifest, but this time *Kaptlt* Reiner Dierksen concluded that the produce bound for the United States constituted contraband. Lundh's visit took twenty minutes, during which time he was treated, in his words, 'with respect and courtesy' before Dierksen made his apologies and ordered the ship sunk. Lundh returned to the freighter and the entire Swedish crew were given thirty minutes to abandon ship in their two lifeboats. The Germans ensured that sufficient

Despite the absence of an air threat, constant vigil had to be maintained towards the clear and distant horizon. On 5 August, at 1430 hours (top), a steamer emerged from the distance and *U 564* took up the chase, Herbert Waldschmidt using the semaphore light to demand that the ship stop or be fired upon.

Artillery and flak crew assembled above decks (centre), ready for action as the distant ship gradually slowed.

In the third photograph Waldschmidt, Lawaetz, Suhren and Wagner (left to right) study their target, ears wadded with cotton wool in anticipation of the warning shot from the 2cm flak weapon.

provisions and navigation equipment were available to the seamen, then *U 176* sank the Swedish ship.[4]

Aboard *U 564*, the interception had at least broken the monotony of the preceding days and provided fresh food for the crew to eat. Teddy headed away from the immediate area but remained close to the prospective rendezvous zone. Kölle's U-boat was sighted a little over an hour later. Suhren, in his autobiography, recalled the meeting:

> We met the captain [Kölle] of the homeward-bound boat at a pre-arranged time and place...By a quirk of fate he turned out to have previously been my divisional officer at Mürwik's Naval Academy, where he had taken such pains to prepare me for the officer's exams. He was the one who had given me the hardest time despite being one of the best. On that day, though, he gazed stupidly at me as I stood there with decorations up to my chin. It was quite a reunion! When I asked him why he was intending to go home with all his torpedoes still on board, he replied that it was because he was ill: he had a liver problem and needed a doctor. 'Oh, I see, belly-ache. Spare me the details. Now let's get the things over here.'

Thereupon the resourceful Teddy and several of his crew stripped off to their underwear and swam across to *U 154* to tie lifejackets to three torpedoes, towing them back by hand. The procedure went

Although the main gun crew assembled on the forward deck and cleared their weapon for action (below left), the 2cm was used to fire the burst across the *Scania* 's bows. As Waldschmidt, Lawaetz and Suhren remain in position on the bridge, a fourth man uses the small chute in the conning tower front that allowed 8.8cm rounds to be passed to the gun crew from the bridge.

The reason for the inability to use the 8.8cm is evident in this photograph (left): forward of the assembled gunners can just be seen the two supporting struts of the torpedo loading cradle. This had already been put into place in anticipation of their rendezvous with Kölle before the steamer's unexpected arrival. Had the gun been fired, the cradle could have cracked under the concussion and been rendered unusable. Small arms have been broken out as well, in preparation for a boarding party to scuttle the ship should she surrender and be deemed an enemy. The barrel of an MP 40 submachine gun is visible

Although Suhren was unlikely to order the 8.8cm gun to fire, the target ship did not know this, and the crew trained their gun on her (right)—clearly visible to lookouts aboard the merchantman and a strong message of intent.

Signalling with flags its compliance, the ship closed down its engines (right) and allowed *U 564* to pull alongside. The flanks of the ship were clearly marked—she was a neutral, the Swedish SS *Scania*.

However, despite her neutral credentials (main illustration), she could still be found to be carrying contraband to a belligerent nation and soon the ship's First Officer was en route to produce the ship's papers for inspection. The Swedish First Officer, Stig Anders August Lundh, was helped aboard *U 564* by the gun crew after first passing up the *Scania*'s manifest and log book.

Lundh was taken to the bridge, where Suhren studied *Scania*'s documents (left, upper). Copenhagen-born Lawaetz was able to converse with Lundh, and the neutral's cargo and course from Bermuda to Buenos Aires was soon confirmed.

Unsure of the wisdom of sinking the Swede, Suhren contented himself with a warning to Lundh that the ship should make no use of its radio and continue on its direct course out of the combat zone (left lower). Interestingly, this photograph was also in Ulrich Gabler's personal collection, which now resides in Altenbruch's U-Boot Archiv. His own humorous interpretation of Teddy's apparent military bearing in this picture is encapsulated in Gabler's handwritten comment beneath it: 'And now, I will sink you!' Fortunately for Lundh, this was not the case, as evidenced by his grin. However, *Scania* would not escape twice from this situation.

As Suhren studied the ship's books, the majority of the U-boats officer's and several crewmen gathered on the bridge (right), all wearing their caps in order to present a more military image than normal. From left are Gabler, Waldschmidt, Hammermüller (with his back to the camera), *Maschinenobergefreiter* Werner Schlägel, Lawaetz, Suhren and Lundh. In the foreground, Heinz Schmutzler keeps the flak weapon trained in the general direction of the Swedish vessel.

smoothly until a fourth torpedo eventually proved too much for the now slightly deflated lifejackets, upending and slipping away to the seabed thousands of metres below. The entire procedure was captured by Haring aboard *U 564* and ironically by another propaganda reporter, Franke, who had gone to sea with Kölle for *U 154*'s dismal patrol.

After also managing to transfer two cubic metres of spare water to *U 564* by dinghy, the two boats parted company and Kölle resumed

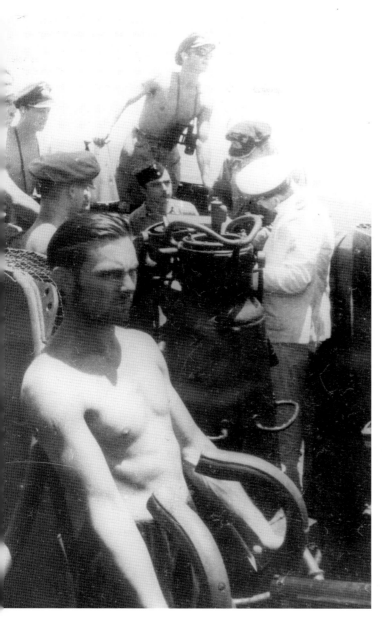

his homeward trek, refuelling again from Wolfbauer. He was welcomed in France with what can be best described as a subdued reception. Kölle, reporting to Dönitz, was relieved of his command and returned to Mürwik. The remainder of *U 154*'s dispirited crew were transferred *en masse* to *U 105*, then in drydock following extensive damage, while *U 105*'s battle-tested complement was given *U 154* in return.

As *U 564* steered towards her patrol area east of the Lesser Antilles — an area shared with *U 66*, *U 108*, *U 155* and *U 160* — five other U-boats were already active to the north, around Florida's east coast and the Greater Antilles. However, the distant Florida boats patrolled initially to little effect among the tropical waters. On 10 August *U 600* attacked and sank a small solo British sailing vessel, the 130-ton *Vivian P. Smith*, but the remainder of the merchant traffic was clustered together in increasingly well-defended convoys. In Florida, *U 98* deposited a minefield in the mouth of Jacksonville harbour — but, again, to no result.

Thus on 10 August, at 0920 hours, as *U 564* lay east of St Lucia and headed south, fresh instructions were received redirecting the boat west-south-west towards ED 90, the grid square centred on Grenada. Teddy would enter the Caribbean after all, but away from the fruitless patrolling of the Greater Antilles boats. Sailing beneath clear skies in a mild and tranquil sea, he was assigned the task of intercepting east-west merchant traffic passing through the Lesser Antilles island chain. He entered his new operational area while submerged, at dawn on 11 August.

At 2118 hours that same day, *U 154* arrived on station and, after a frosty meeting between commanders, the transfer of torpedoes began as rehearsed by *U 564*'s crew. This and the following images, taken from *U 154*, appear to have been captured by another photographer, Franke, aboard Kölle's boat; Haring recorded their labours on film from Teddy's point of view. As before, dinghies were also used to transfer spare fresh water to *U 564*. The block and tackle and wide decking of the larger Type IX boat is clearly depicted in this photograph, as the first torpedo is about to be lowered into the sea.

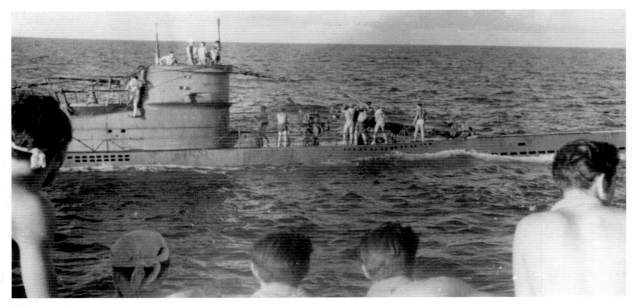

Repeating the same procedure as before, three torpedoes were successfully taken aboard *U 564* (left). Unfortunately for Suhren, the fourth went to the bottom as the lifejackets had lost some of their buoyancy during the nearly five hours it took to complete the operation.

(Right) In mild seas and good visibility, *U 564* continued west. During the voyage, the diesel engines passed their 10,000,000th revolution, prompting a small celebration. In the photograph below, Gabler pours a small glass of schnapps for Eberhard Hammer-müller; *ObMsch* Kräh waits his turn. Joined by Helmut Brock, the four men celebrate the milestone passed by *U 564* 's engines (bottom).

5 War off the Antilles

12 TO 19 AUGUST

U564 had surfaced a little past 0100 hours in order to begin her Caribbean patrol. Lawaetz and his three men took their usual positions atop the small conning tower and scoured the seas for shipping—or for the detritus left behind careless merchantmen that could betray their path. Rubbish thoughtlessly jettisoned overboard could leave a traceable path for a lucky U-boat, and anything sighted within the gentle swell was scrutinised intently. But the hours passed with no sign of friend or foe. Finally, at 0755 hours, as Waldschmidt's watch was drawing to a close and Limburg's men ate a hurried breakfast before taking over on the bridge, a distant shadow was sighted dead ahead.

Although German time held aboard the U-boat indicated that the sun should be well above the horizon, it was still only 0355 hours local time and the sea was cloaked in darkness. The shadow hardened into an identifiable enemy, and Teddy came rapidly to the bridge to decide what course of action should be taken. His men, standing to at Action Stations, waited in hushed anticipation for orders from their captain. But the small vessel that crossed their path

A submerging Second World War U-boat was at its most vulnerable to surface attack, particularly by aircraft. Speed was of the essence. In these photographs once again (below), with the diving alarm sounded, Labahn and Abel close exhaust vents, shut off the diesels and engage the electric motors. Nearing the combat zone, *U 564* was once more compelled to travel increasingly long distances underwater owing, in the main, to the threat posed by enemy aircraft.

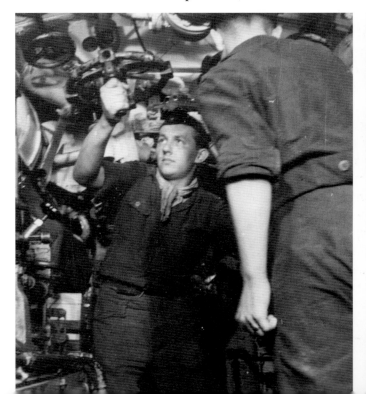

On 10 August *U 564* received a revised operating area from BdU centred on the island of Grenada. Here Rudi Elkerhausen, Senior Radio Petty Officer, decodes the message using the four-rotor 'Enigma'. He would later transmit his boat's brief confirmation and situation report.

at considerable range was an American patrol craft — not worthy of a torpedo in Teddy's estimation. However, the encounter had served to highlight their arrival in the combat zone, and his crew congratulated themselves on their vigilance. *U 564* quietly changed course away from the threat and carried on the hunt, submerging to rest the lookouts with the coming of dawn.

All day the U-boat sailed steadily north-west towards Grenada. Early the following afternoon, a distant aircraft was sighted; two hours later, another was caught through binoculars. Suhren had added an extra man to each watch, the fifth pair of eyes devoted solely to guarding against enemy aircraft attack. The seeming regularity of the enemy aerial patrols did not, however, allow the lookouts to spot a third aircraft at 1936 hours — a large, four-engine bomber diving towards *U 564* from out of the blazing, late-afternoon Caribbean sun. With only seconds to spare, Waldschmidt shouted for a crash-dive, slammed the main hatch shut behind him and plummeted to the Control Room floor, *U 564* tilting downwards as the alarm claxon shrilled its warning throughout the boat. The aircraft passed almost directly overhead, dropping two depth charges wide of the mark as the U-boat raced for depth and safety. It had been a near miss for the lucky crew, but once again they had escaped unscathed.

Elsewhere that same day, 13 August, in the Windward Passage, *U 658* sighted two converging convoys shuttling via Curaçao between Key West and Trinidad. The southbound WAT.13 and northbound TAW.12 totalled 47 ships. Attacking WAT.13, the crew of *U 658* were rewarded with three explosions and sighted flames, a stern shot also appearing to strike its target although only one ship was confirmed sunk by the Allied reports. Zurmühlen's *U 600* joined battle against TAW.12, hitting the *Everelza* and sending her under beneath a column of flame hundreds of metres high. A second attack sank the American convoy commodore aboard SS *Delmundo*. Yet another boat arrived to savage the convoy, Gottfried Holtorf in *U 598* sinking three ships on 14 August before TAW.12 arrived in Key West.

As the Morse messages crackled from U-boats engaging the enemy within the Windward Passage, Teddy's radio men intercepted the calls of victory and loss, decrypting the communication between the fighting boats and BdU in Paris. Although the combat raged some hundreds of miles from their present position, Suhren monitored developments closely, awaiting his own specific instructions from headquarters. However, while his comrades tussled with the enemy, Suhren encountered only a solitary ship during 14 August, frustratingly a neutral Argentinean clearly identified and allowed to pass unmolested.

On 16 August, after two days of irritating limbo, Suhren radioed his situation reports to BdU, asking for further directions. At 0457 hours he again lost patience with the stubborn silence from Dönitz and ordered a message transmitted bemoaning the fact that, since 12 August, between the squares ED9417, 9883, 9527 and 9892 and

Beneath the harsh glare of a tropical sun, exposed metal can become extremely hot and inflict mild burns on those who touch it with bare flesh. The wooden panelling that Richard Steinert is leaning against here (above left) prevented just such an injury, the crumpled towel in the background ready for his use if he wanted to perch on the conning-tower rim.

War and peace: *U 564*'s lookouts beneath the tranquillity of a Caribbean summer evening (above right).

The first call to Action Stations for August was on the 12th, when AN American escort vessel passed at a distance. However, Suhren deemed it not worth a torpedo. He patrolled until 19 August, suffering sporadic air attacks and sighting only a single neutral before latching on to convoy TAW(S) on 19 August. Two surface attacks were launched, followed by a third submerged. Here (below left), Gerhard Ehlers stands ready to fire tube 1. Lifejackets are worn by the crew during combat. Assisting Ehlers is the boat's cook, Hausruckinger (below right). *U 564* was short by two crewmen after the loss of Schlittenhard and Grade, and, although normally excused other duties, Hausruckinger played an important part in combat as he had on previous cruises, when he had been the second cook.

cruising with extended aircraft watches, they had seen nothing worth shooting at. Finally, at 0513 hours, both Suhren and Wattenberg's *U 162* were assigned the western length of ED9880 — north of Trinidad — as their attack area. Still *U 564* found nothing but empty seas. The easy pickings amongst crowded Caribbean shipping lanes that had begun with the first U-boat attacks in the region only the previous February were already a faded memory.

Sailing close to the Allied airfields on Trinidad carried its own inherent risk. A distant aircraft was sighted on 17 August at 1340 hours and warily tracked until out of sight. Beneath the blistering sun, the lookouts were stripped to the waist and shaded only by their large tropical helmets. Polarised sunglasses helped to reduce the fierce glare of the sun's rays reflecting off the azure waters, but the four-hour shifts of scanning a bare distant horizon and sky stretched the men's abilities to their limit.

At 2050, in ED8641, the startled cry that the entire crew dreaded to hear burst from the bridge: '*Flieger!*' A large enemy aircraft was closing rapidly from out of the sun, flattening out only twenty metres above the waves and heading rapidly into a low-level attack. Throwing the boat into its practised crash-dive routine, Gabler took her down as fast as possible, *U 564* reaching such an acute angle that loose fixtures of all descriptions tumbled from their place and

clattered noisily toward the bow. With mere metres of water over her bridge, three well-placed bombs bracketed the U-boat, severely shaking the hull and causing fresh chaos aboard. A thin jet of flame shot from the closed hatch to number five torpedo tube, prompting considerable alarm amongst the men who saw it as they manned the electric motors and diesel engines. However, there was no water leakage and the engineers could only assume that, though the tube may have been damaged by the bomb blasts, it remained watertight. Machine-gun fire peppered the water above *U 564*, although more to vent the Allied gunners' frustration than with any real hope of hitting the target. The aircraft's final throw of the dice hit *U 564* at a depth of 40 metres when a single heavy depth charge exploded perilously close to Teddy's boat and caused heavy damage. Men were nearly thrown from their feet, and *U 564* staggered under the impact. Lights shattered and broken glass tinkled to the decking, un-

Hermann Kräh times the torpedo run within his diesel room (below left). The first bow salvo missed, the second ending in a twin detonation of exploding warheads an hour after the opening attack. Chased from the scene of the two burning ships by escort vessels, the dogged Suhren attempted a third submerged attack as the sun arced overhead (below right). Ulrich Gabler sits at his Action Station behind the two planesmen within the Control Room (opposite left). The bow planes (at left) are being controlled by Heinrich Bartels, the stern planes by Heinz Schmutzler. Above Bartels' head, the boat's depth gauge shows 18 metres, with bow planes on full rise as he arrests the descent and

heard amidst the cacophony of disturbed water that pummelled the pressure hull. Suhren held his men under firm control, his quiet authority and unshakable calm keeping in check any distress felt by his crew. Questions regarding the status of their pressure hull's watertight integrity flashed from the Control Room and returned from all quarters with a reassuring negative: there were no leaks.

An atmosphere of professional calm descended over the crew, and the required bravado at another narrow shave with death passed among the men still lying where they had tumbled within the U-boat's bow compartment. In the Control Room, Gabler began to bring *U 564* to trim and reported the depth as 60 metres. But, within seconds, both he and Suhren realised that something had indeed gone terribly wrong.

Alongside the normal noises generated by the boat were strong echoing creaks and groans that shuddered through *U 564*'s sturdy

frames. To an experienced U-boat man, the distinctive noises could mean only one thing: they were plummeting downwards into the immense water pressure of extreme depth. The fear of slipping silently into the abyss until the pressure hull imploded suddenly gripped the entire crew, and Teddy ordered both planes on hard rise and forward tanks blown clear of ballast with compressed air. The boat's descent must be stopped, her bows forced to rise if they were ever to regain the surface. Panicking, the seaman responsible for operating the complicated blowing panel had mistakenly turned his hand wheels the wrong way, achieving nothing until Teddy dashed across the Control Room and spun them fully open. Gabler had abandoned his obviously faulty gauge and soon discovered, using the trim cell gauge, that their depth was 160 metres — ten metres below the boat's shipyard rated test depth — and growing deeper.

As compressed air hissed through pipes and into the ballast tanks, within another twenty metres the freefall gradually tapered off and the bow perceptibly began to rise towards the horizontal. *U 564*'s freefall had been arrested at a depth of 200

metres, every frame screaming with the strain, but no visible leaks were found. An absolute hush descended over the entire boat as Gabler gingerly eased them away from the sea floor thousands of metres below. *U 564* gently ascended to a safer depth, and before long the engineering crew set about repairing the many systems that had taken damage, thanking their good fortune at sailing aboard a boat built in Hamburg. Gabler disassembled his main depth gauge to discover that the pointer had come adrift from its small drive shaft during the concussion of the last depth charge. It had remained set at 60 metres, and would have stayed there as the U-boat slipped into oblivion.

Several delicate instruments attached to the hull plates had been torn loose from their mountings by the attack and bulbs and other

Also inside the cramped conning tower during the submerged attack, *Bootsmann* Heinz Webendörfer stands at his attack station and enters information into the torpedo computer (above and above centre). This analogue system transmitted information about the U-boat and target's range, speed, bearing and heading to enable the necessary firing solution to be calculated. Any alterations could then be automatically tracked by the computer, the required information transmitted electronically to the torpedoes in their tubes. In this case it was to no avail, both

torpedoes fired hitting their targets but failing to explode.
Heinz Schmutzler decorates Teddy's slippers (above right), less to celebrate the patrol being half over than to help his captain identify his left from his right when called unexpectedly from his bunk to the Control Room!

glass panels needed replacing. Despite some scepticism from their commander following the report of a jet of flame from the closed torpedo hatch, tube five had indeed suffered damage and was temporarily flooded. Prudently keeping his boat submerged, Teddy supervised the flurry of repair activity within, relieved with the realisation that no serious damage had been inflicted. He reasoned that conditions were less than ideal for lookouts forced to endure hours of baking heat and still detect any threat of enemies from the sun, and so chose to place his faith in the boat's hydrophones, which gave superb performance in the ethereal blue water. However, although the deep offered temporary safety and the ability to relax for much of the crew, it remained damp and humid within the steel tube, sweat running from every pore of the weary men:

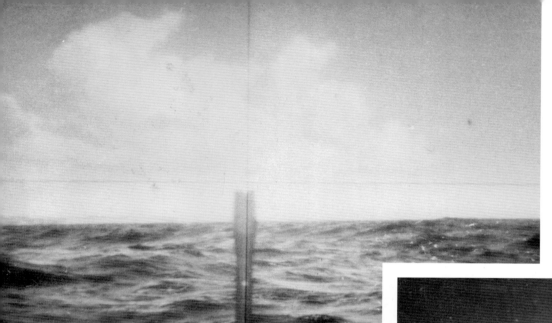

> After the engines had run at high speed, we used to find it so hot in the Caribbean Sea that even when we were under water the temperature in the submarine reached up to 60 degrees, which made it very uncomfortable for the whole crew. But, even then, we made it possible to bring them all back to the mainland without having lost too much weight.[1]

As *U 564* picked up the pieces and sailed submerged from the scene of its latest brush with the enemy, that same day *U 658* attacked convoy PG.6 south of Cuba, sinking two of the 23 ships sailing under American escort and damaging a third. The Caribbean battle continued to rage with renewed vigour from both sides.

With all systems restored aboard *U 564* by 18 August, including the full use of the stern torpedo tube, and the boat once again ready to spend time above the waves, a message from Scholtz's *U 108* was received at 1043 hours reporting the longed-for heavy convoy traffic within striking range of *U 564*. Scholtz had chanced upon TAW(S), comprising fifteen merchant ships escorted by the corvettes HMS *Clarkia* and USS *Courage*, the US Coast Guard cutters *Marion* and *Antietam* and the US submarine-chasers *PC-482*, *PC-492*, *SC-504* and *SC-514*. With an almost constant shadow overhead of locally stationed American B-18 and British Hudson bombers,

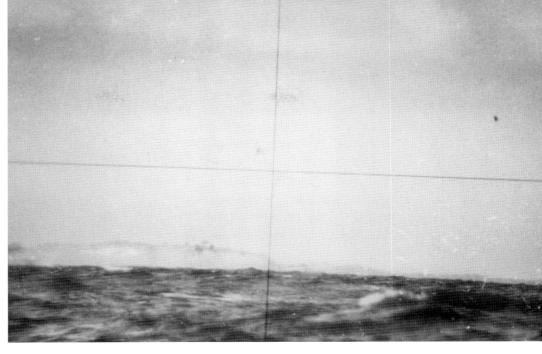

The sun-baked cliffs of Point Saline mark the southernmost promontory of Grenada (right) as *U 564* sails slowly seaward of the shallow, banking reef system offshore. Point Saline's lighthouse was an important navigational aid to shipping transiting the southern entrance to the Caribbean; another navigational radio beacon, at Pearls Airport on the island's east coast, was used for air traffic via the Caribbean to points in West Africa and South America.

the feeder convoy TAW(S) had departed Trinidad that day on the first leg of a journey to Key West and, ultimately, the United Kingdom. After growing considerably in size, the final conglomeration of extra ships was intended to join out of Halifax, Nova Scotia, and, receiving an HX number, the convoy would end its voyage in Great Britain carrying priceless cargo for the Allied build-up taking place within the embattled island. Wattenberg had also begun to shadow, while BdU threw the attack open to any nearby boats. *U 564* rose to the challenge.

The boat surged forward with renewed vigour; her torpedoes were run out of their tubes and checked for possible faults, while a myriad other systems were tested and retested, using to its utmost the time available before the expected contact. Once their tasks were complete, men who had no further duties were ordered to rest in preparation for the exertion that would soon follow. Awaiting further developments from Scholtz, Suhren was rewarded with fresh information on 19 August at 0315 hours when the radio crackled with news from *U 162* of the convoy's latest position: 'KR KR; convoy in grid ED 9460, northeasterly course, steady speed, Wattenberg.

Only 35 nautical miles from the reported position, Suhren accelerated to intercept, Wattenberg's *U 162* beginning her own surface attack a little over an hour later at 0437 hours (1137 hours local time) and sinking the American SS *West Celina* with a two-torpedo shot near Grenada. Above the bewildered merchantmen, the sky erupted in the phosphorescent glare of starshell as ships swerved to avoid collision with the *West Celina*, the entire convoy veering away to port of their previous track and away from the direction of the torpedo attack. Above them, the Hudson bomber plummeted on to the vague outline of Wattenberg's boat, betrayed by the swinging parachute flares, harassing *U 162* until Wattenberg was forced to break away and retreat submerged.

At 0630 hours the glaring lights of the distress flares became visible to starboard of *U 564*, eighty-five miles north-west of Boca Grande, Trinidad. Teddy ordered course to be altered, and ten minutes later sighted the squat shadows of laden ships. The smudges on the horizon quickly hardened into the convoy's profile, and periodic flares continued to cast an unnatural glow over the scene, the escort ships and aircraft attempting to dissuade any further surfaced U-boats from approaching. Teddy carefully pondered his best approach as he stalked from the darkness of the opposite beam to that which Wattenberg had attacked from.

After nearly half an hour of deliberation with his officers atop the U-boat's bridge, Teddy ordered his men to Battle Stations and began his surface run into the attack. Lawaetz manned the UZO as diesels pounded and the U-boat surged through the water. But the sudden and unexpected appearance of an enemy escort's slim silhouette caused the German attackers to fire from a greater distance than planned: five single shots were loosed at the distant merchant ships as *U 564* swung to port and raced from the enemy, its final torpedo arcing away from the stern tube. Stopwatches began counting off the seconds till impact, but, to the dismay of the entire crew, it was soon discovered that they had fired prematurely, missing the targets after misjudging their distance, with the torpedoes streaking away into the darkness behind the convoy.

Thus, as *U 564* retreated to the east, the arduous task of reloading four tubes began again. Ehlers and his torpedo crew raced to lift the stored 'eels' from the bilge, hoisting them with chains and pulleys on to the loading beams. Quickly greased and inspected within their delicate balance chambers for any defects, the deadly cylinders were run into the tubes and made ready to fire.

One by one, the small bulbs on the torpedo panel flickered into life and by 0900 hours, barely an hour after the last attack, the boat was cleared for action, tubes one to three and the stern tube, No 5, ready to fire. It took a further hour for Suhren to place himself in what he considered the ideal firing position before *U 564* began her second run-in. With the escort ships well to the convoy's front and an exposed flank beckoning to him, Suhren waited until his targets were at a range of 1,000 metres and properly overlapping. Four ships were selected: two large tankers estimated to be worth 8,000 tons each; one large freighter of 7,000 tons and an average-size ship of 5,000 tons — one torpedo for each. While Lawaetz again manned the UZO and lined the targeting device's crosshairs on each consecutive objective, Teddy gave the order to shoot. Lawaetz let loose a new barrage at 1007 hours. The first two tubes fired almost simultaneously, followed by tube three a minute later. The last to be launched was that from the stern tube, almost another two minutes after the last shot and not until the U-boat had again been sent into a high-speed turn, swinging around so that the final shot could be made once more as they began their escape:

> All four torpedoes hit as targeted. Two ships sank quickly, but it was impossible to tell at the time whether one was a tanker or freighter. The other tanker, glowing bright red with an internal explosion, at first made a slow getaway as if to wait for the sinking of the two other ships. [Then she] quickly sank to the sternposts and [was] . . . up to the bridge in water.

Suddenly an enemy escort began to take up the chase, aided by what Teddy took to be a British flying boat overhead. He ordered that a rapid report be despatched to BdU that two tankers and two large freighters had been hit, totalling 28,000 tons — two confirmed sunk and two left in a sinking condition — finishing by reporting himself under pursuit by a 'destroyer' and a flying boat. In fact, Suhren had hit and sunk two only of the targeted ships during his attack. The tanker SS *British Consul* and the freighter SS *Empire Cloud* had both staggered under the blow of torpedo impact and were slumping low into the water, the tanker immediately beginning to sink.

Ironically, both had been hit by German torpedoes before. On 19 February 1942 the *British Consul* had been at anchor in the harbour at

Port of Spain, Trinidad, when *Kaptlt.* Albrecht Achilles had launched a daring night-time surface attack within the closely guarded harbour. Achilles hit two of the ships, the American steamer SS *Mokihana* and the *British Consul*. However, despite the double sinking, both vessels settled on the shallow, silty harbour floor, where fires on board were soon extinguished, and both were later salvaged and returned to service.[2] The second of Teddy's victims, the SS *Empire Cloud*, had been badly damaged by torpedoes from 'Adi' Schnee's *U 201* in May 1941 but had been abandoned and towed by the Dutch tug *Thames* into Reykjavik, returned to Greenock and repaired.

Suhren's torpedoes struck both ships almost at the same time, the eighteen-year-old *British Consul* taking two into her heavily loaded hull. Two men were killed instantly in the deafening initial blast, and the ship's master, James Kennedy, ordered his vessel abandoned by the forty remaining crewmen, the gunners and the single passenger. Fortunately for them, HMS *Clarkia* unhesitatingly closed the fortunate survivors and hauled them aboard to safety.[3] Behind them, the 6,940-ton tanker buckled and went to the bottom, carrying with her a valuable cargo of Trinidadian oil that had been bound for the United Kingdom.

Master Charles Cottew Brown's SS *Empire Cloud* had also taken casualties from the blast. Three men lost their lives within the merchantman's hull as water flooded through the hole ripped in her side by *U 564*. This was a brand new ship, completed only the previous year as a part of the same emergency buying or building 'Empire' programme which had produced the *Empire Hawksbill* that Suhren had sunk from OS.34. Brown ordered his crew and the eight gunners carried aboard the 5,969-ton ship to prepare to abandon *Empire Cloud* as she listed dangerously and began to settle. The shipwrecked survivors were gathered up by other convoy members, scattered between two different ships and very thankful to have not been left behind.[4] However, once again, the *Empire Cloud* refused to go under. A Dutch tug based in Trinidad, the *Roode Zee*, later attempted to tow the stricken vessel back to Port of Spain, but she eventually foundered on 21 August.

Heinz Nordmann takes advantage of one of the unusual features installed aboard *U 564* — a shower. 'At the back of the diesel room one could remove the floorboards and into that space they built a bath, just big enough for one to sit in and also to have a shower. We were able to have a shower with the warm water of the [engine] cooling system. In those days we had seawater soap . . . a marvellous idea!'

Making a high-speed surface dash to sanctuary, Suhren managed to escape into the blanketing darkness, and the pursuing escort ship soon gave up the chase. But the aircraft did not, and *U 564* was finally forced under at 1050 hours by a B-18 bomber that ran in from the darkened heavens to fly close alongside, apparently in preparation for an attack. The racket of the alarm claxon reverberated through the boat, flashing lights within the diesel room showing Kräh and his crew that the engines needed to be stopped immediately and all valves opened to enable the boat to race for safety underwater. With practised ease, *U 564* hurtled below, the slim hull arrowing downwards and away from her aerial tormentor. Within the dripping hull, the German crew could hear the unmistakable and chilling sound of bulkheads collapsing aboard the SS *British Consul* as the tanker headed for the seabed. The rending of torn iron and steel echoed through the dense seawater and among the underwater canyons, bringing surprisingly little joy to the U-boat's crew, despite their triumph. The sound represented a disturbing reminder of the fate of any vessel that lost its battle for survival during the bitter war at sea.

There was a momentary burst of frantic activity as *U 564* ducked under the water, her screws thrashing their way through the calm surface and pushing the U-boat at full speed downwards. The forward hydroplane operator was unable to arrest the descent when Gabler asked planes to be set to level, having to heave on the emergency wheel that surrounded his push-button mechanism. Slowly, the boat sinking ten metres every thirty seconds, the hydroplanes began to work free of the momentary jam and *U 564* eased out of her downward plunge, finally to be brought to trim at fifty metres.

After spending only fifteen minutes running submerged, Teddy hoped to have thrown the enemy off his scent and ordered hydroplanes on rise and his boat surfaced once again. Now the flying boat was further away, scanning the Caribbean waters several miles forward of *U 564*'s bow. But, with darkness still shrouding the scene, Teddy reasoned that he could slip away still surfaced and ordered full speed as he crossed the convoy's wake, pounding just out of sight over the horizon on the freighters' starboard flank and speeding ahead to position himself once again within firing range of the path of the oncoming depleted convoy.

With the breaking of the brief equatorial dawn at 1130 hours (0630 hours local time), *U 564* dived to periscope depth, the steamers predictably wallowing in a straight line from the north-west and passing before Teddy's submerged boat, allowing a perfect underwater attack. Slowly the merchantmen plodded into his field of fire, their great lazy screws providing the familiar slow, rhythmic pulse through the water, until at 1356 hours, with his targets only 20 degrees off the starboard bow, Teddy commenced his third attempted attack, this time launching his last two wakeless electric torpedoes in broad daylight.

At a depth of 13.5 metres, and with the pair of chosen targets passing at a range of only 500m and 600m, Suhren ordered tubes 1 and 2 fired. With such ideal positioning and slow-moving ships, Teddy must have felt almost assured of success. But, after only 59 seconds the sound of an unexploded torpedo striking metal was plainly audible, not only through the hydrophone gear but also to the naked ear within the U-boat's hull. Twenty seconds later a second metallic strike was heard, the *whirr* of the torpedo's small propeller cut abruptly short. Both torpedoes had struck their targets, but they had been duds. Teddy fumed as he looked once more through his periscope, the first of his targets briefly stopped before re-joining the convoy and continuing unmolested. The irritated captain later recorded his weapons failure for a radio message to BdU:

> [Torpedo] courses were right for the estimated distance. Settings 73degs, depth 3m. Pistol detonator numbers 27908, 32077, both from leaded containers . . . Short metallic strike and after that no torpedo noise in the hydrophone. One steamer stopped briefly.
>
> Still two Atos, set off to load them in the 'Scholtz' area [south-east of Grenada]. 98cbm. Contact broken off. Last position at 1600hrs, ED8392, course 315degs, speed 7 knots. Still 11 ships. Remaining at ED9424. Suhren.

After creeping away from the convoy for two hours, Teddy Suhren brought his boat once again to the surface to send his last contact and status report and attempt to put some distance between himself and his enemy in order to facilitate the downloading of the final remaining exterior stowed torpedo. The distant convoy could still be seen from the boat, and the ever-present aircraft continued to circle above. Once again, this bane of the German submariner made an unwelcome appearance above *U 564*, flying directly for Teddy's boat and forcing yet another crash-dive to safety. No depth charges followed, but shortly afterwards the distinctive sound of approaching propellers heralded the arrival of two small patrol vessels to hound the suspected U-boat beneath them, guided to the spot by the aircraft. Fearing the worst, Suhren's crew were visibly relieved when still no depth charges followed, the two ships not being equipped with ASDIC and thus unable to locate *U 564*. Still, their presence was enough to dissuade further action during daylight as they lingered above the slowly moving U-boat until 2200 hours before gradually moving away from the scene.

Despite Teddy's unintentionally inflated claims regarding sinkings, his attack had still been relatively successful against this, the only TAW(S) convoy to be hit by U-boats during the war. However, it had taken eleven torpedoes, hauled first by train from Kiel to Brest then by U-boat from occupied France across the Atlantic Ocean, to achieve the destruction of two ships—hardly the most economical success rate.

As *U 564* cruised slowly away from the scene of her latest struggle, the majority of the crew took the opportunity to unwind. With a single compressed-air torpedo quickly loaded into tube No 1, and no further torpedoes available within the hull, the task of reloading the final externally stored 'eel' would have to wait and the decision to surface in secrecy and safety postponed to allow time to complete the task. Suhren also used the period to further advantage, writing general notations in his War Diary about his experience of Caribbean operations. The comments, like those made by all commanders at sea, would later prove invaluable to Dönitz, enabling him to attempt to perceive a 'first-hand' feel of the battle at sea.

U-boats must stay dived by day, so as to remain unseen at all costs. They need to try to attack as often as possible during the first night, since it is almost impossible to maintain contact on subsequent days, due to the bright nights as well as small patrol boats. There is considerable danger of being bombed here by fast 'tractors'.

If there are too many boats in the convoy to be sunk, then a chosen U-boat must move at top speed so as to get in the convoy's path three hours before dawn. This boat then needs to travel underwater at three to four knots in the same direction as the convoy's course, so that it will have a good vantage point for the convoy three to four hours before dusk. The crew can relax during the other daylight hours . . .

This method of keeping in contact can only hold good for suitable sea areas, and could be successfully employed with one of the convoys coming out of the Strait of Gibraltar. The [delegated] U-boat needs then, as a matter of course, to abandon an attack [in order to move ahead].

The safety of the convoy is assured by air cover, sea cover being relatively weak. Once the convoy is spotted, set a course at the furthest possible point from which it is visible and for thirty minutes take a parallel course with a speed which allows you to overtake the enemy . . .

Above the convoy, the planes have lights fitted, and on their circuits obviously travel over the boat. Since, however, [their] night vision is the same as [ours], always keep sufficient distance. Then, at the edge of visibility, turn so that the convoy is at 0 degrees. With a running fix, mount the attack from ahead.

When the plane approaches, the boat must still move forward a little in the water and keep this up until the plane leaves the area. The aircraft will always first throw a starshell, since till then it does not know whether it is dealing with the white spray around one of its own patrol boats.

Once the ships are as far as possible all overlapping, shoot, turn and run. Save the next freighter in line for the stern tube.

With hindsight, it can be seen that, by the time of Teddy's departure from the Caribbean battleground, the fickle fortunes of war had already turned against Germany's submariners within the tropics. The Allies' increasingly effective air power, their freshly introduced centimetric radar, their growing escort strength and their hard-won experience were irretrievably altering the balance of power in their favour. The cramped confines of the Caribbean soon became too risky for high concentrations of U-boats, and by early September those still in the region were moved towards Trinidad and further east to the junction of the Trinidad and New York convoy routes. The narrow chokepoints linking the Atlantic with the Caribbean that U-boats had initially used against their merchant prey now worked against them, since Allied power was able to smother over the slender passages and render them extremely hazardous for U-boat penetration.

6 Artillery Attack, Promotion, Home

20 AUGUST TO 18 SEPTEMBER

U *564* continued to travel mainly submerged by day, owing to the threat posed by enemy aircraft. Inside the submarine, the temperature soared as the boat lay at depth within the warm Caribbean Sea. As dusk arrived, Teddy would bring the boat to the surface to change the fetid air within the hull and allow the depleted batteries to be charged by diesel-driven generators. The appearance of two distant freighters and a single corvette escort triggered an alarm-dive on 21 August. Teddy studied the situation by periscope, but realised that the target was too far away to intercept.

It was not until late that night that he deemed the area secure enough to allow the block-and-tackle rigged to remove the last stored torpedo from its container below the hardwood decking. Beneath an idyllic tropical night sky, the crew laboured for seventy minutes to free the cumbersome 'eel' from its compartment, opening the forward loading hatch and lowering it gently inside the hull, where it was manoeuvred into tube two. The last pair of 'eels' were ready to fire, and Suhren cruised towards the south-east from Grenada, passing the latter's southern tip during the day and even allowing Haring to attach his Leica camera to the navigation periscope and photograph Point Salines and the sweep of the bay in which nestled the island's capital, St George's.

Behind St George's were the only two major gun emplacements on the island, the first at Richmond Hill, now the site of Grenada's prison, the other at Ross Point. However, the batteries offered little more than psychological comfort for the local Commonwealth populace, the Southern Caribbean Defence Force having been instructed not to fire on any sighted U-boats for fear of retaliation. In any event, they lacked sufficient firepower to do so effectively, even if permitted.

With priority again on target acquisition, U 564 spent more time travelling surfaced, bringing upon herself another air attack on 24 August as the boat was thrown into a crash-dive when lookouts spotted the approaching threat. Five depth charges chased them below, but they caused little damage. A second alarm-dive only five minutes after resurfacing forced a rethink, and Teddy elected to depart the area submerged once more, daring to surface only after several hours had passed.

The tropical heat was beginning to inflict the inevitable detrimental effects on those men who were largely confined below decks. Rashes and sores made their belated appearance, although Suhren was determined to avoid the appalling conditions often found aboard a combat boat:

> We also made sure of hygiene, which was difficult. The men didn't receive a lot of water to wash themselves with. They grew beards, and none of this helped cleanliness. So then our chief engineer (Gabler) and his diesel officer (Kräh) decided that something had to be done. At the back of the diesel room one could remove the floor boards, and into that space they built a bath, just big enough for one to sit in and also to have a shower. We were able to have a shower with the warm water of the [engine] cooling system. In those days we had seawater soap . . . a marvellous idea! All we had to do now was to keep check on who was due, and then everyone received a litre of fresh water to finally rinse himself off with. That paid off very well, because the crew, even in this tremendous heat, felt very comfortable. We also had on board a freshwater producer, but it took one litre of diesel to produce one litre of freshwater.[1]

As *U 564* continued her hunt, on 25 August the crew's patience appeared to be rewarded when signals were received from Wattenberg aboard *U 162*: 'Heavy NE–SW traffic moving on shipping route near quads 72–82. Air cover.' This was the lead that Teddy had needed, and *U 564* altered course to the north-east in order to converge upon Wattenberg's reported traffic. Elsewhere, near Haiti and off the Virgin Islands, U-boats were reporting scattered successes, and it was not long before Wattenberg did the same. An updated message arrived during 26 August: 'Heavy traffic in EE 5773 and 5781 observed. Yesterday two fast ships EE 57, course SW hunted in vain.' But Wattenberg's next attack yielded fruit, and he was soon able to report the sinking of the SS *Thelma*.

Meanwhile Teddy's inability to find potential targets forced him to retrace his steps westwards before swinging towards Tobago in search of what, in his report to BdU, he called a 'new goldmine'. It was not long in coming.

During the early hours of the penultimate day of August, but still before midnight local time,

With only two air-driven torpedoes remaining after the struggle against TAW (S), Suhren elected to take *U 564* to the east of the Windward Isles and wait astride what was known as the 'Scholz' route for merchant shipping. During the darkness of early morning on 30 August *U 564* attacked its final target, the MV *Vardaas*. The battle took place in darkness, but these photographs of an artillery practice shoot illustrate the method of attack. Here (below) Richard Steinert emerges from the tower as part of the gun crew.

U 564 cruised in conditions reminiscent of a stereotypical picture postcard. A gentle easterly wind barely brushed the water, the sea state reduced to quiet undulations that did no more than gently rock the boat as she sailed north-east of Tobago. A thin layer of cloud passed periodically in front of the bright moonlight that allowed excellent visibility to the men on watch. During the periodic sweep of binoculars over the distant horizon, one small area of shadow to starboard, darker than the surrounding night, began to materialise. Calling Teddy to the bridge, Waldschmidt studied the distant shadow conferring with his captain and bringing the boat on to a potential intercept course. Gradually the shape hardened into the unmistakable silhouette of a solo sailing tanker, her long hull riding high in the Caribbean waters, betraying a ship travelling in ballast. *U 564* was put into high speed as Teddy brought the boat arcing to starboard and placed her at right angles to the tanker's general course.

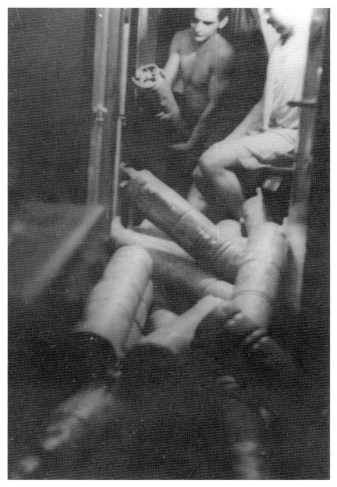

Shortly after arriving at his chosen position, Teddy was compelled to dive, the ambient moonlight being too bright to allow a successful surfaced approach. Fortunately for him, the unwitting merchantman was making regular ten-minute zigzags at right angles to her course, and one such alteration would bring her headed on an unwavering line directly before *U 564*'s torpedo tubes.

The ship that Suhren was tracking through his attack periscope was the 8,176-ton, Kiel-built, Norwegian MT *Vardaas*. Captained by Hans Rustad, the large tanker had been in Admiralty service since 1940 as a part of the Royal Fleet Auxiliary after the fall of Norway to the Germans. *Vardaas* had spent most of spring 1942 engaged in transporting oil from the British naval base at Trincomalee, Ceylon,

Another photograph (far left) of Kräh and Bigge were involved in bringing the 8.8cm ammunition from below the decks.

Once unpacked, the shells were passed man from man through the boat and out of the conning tower. There they were put on to a small slide to the outer deck level.

On deck, the ammunition was retrieved by the loaders (lsft). To the right is Richard Steinert, to the left the boat's cook, Hermann Hausruckinger. With the absence of Ernst Schlittenhard from the gun crew, Hausruckinger resumed the duty that he had undertaken as part of the crew before his transfer to the post of boat's chef during this cruise.

to Colombo, always sailing without escort. The last time the crew had entered Colombo, on Easter morning, they had suffered damage during a Japanese air attack, strafed repeatedly although not attacked with bombs and suffering no casualties and only minor damage.

Now her voyage from Cape Town to Trinidad was to end dramatically, as at 0612 hours Teddy ordered the first of his last pair of air torpedoes to be fired. The tanker had just completed one of her predictable changes of course, heading 230 degrees, when the G7a in tube No 2 was ejected from the U-boat and began its final journey. Teddy had estimated that it should hit in less than a minute, and thirty seconds after launch the dull rumble of an exploding torpedo resounded through the water. It was a direct hit.

Raising his periscope up for a quick look at his quarry, Teddy could plainly see men racing for their lifeboat stations, the ship swinging lazily to port as her screw stopped revolving, although she appeared to be neither burning nor sinking. But with such obvious distress there seemed little danger, and *U 564* was brought to the surface to administer the *coup de grâce*. Cautiously, Teddy edged his boat nearer in preparation for a final broadside shot, watching warily for any sign of gunners attempting to man the single, stern-mounted artillery piece. Oddly, there was no distress message from the hapless tanker—something that her master would later be harshly criticised for. Within ten minutes, the entire thirty-nine-man crew and her two British gunners had abandoned the *Vardaas* and left her to drift

Standing at right with his back to the camera is *Bootsmann* Heinz Webendörfer (main illustration). He was chief of the gun crew on deck and occupied the starboard ranging sight—one of two either side and the only one clipped in place during this shoot.
(Inset) Hausruckinger prepares to ram his shell home into the breech.

listlessly in the gentle swell. By then, as the lifeboats pulled clear, Teddy had already elected to use his final 'eel' to destroy the ship, diving to make another submerged attack. Carefully lining up his target, he ordered the torpedo launched and Ehlers hammered down on the firing handle. To the alarm of all hands within the forward torpedo room, the unmistakable sound of the torpedo's small propellers pierced the silence, penetrating through the tube itself. The torpedo was a 'hot runner' and had somehow snagged itself within the tube, the small compressed air motor bursting into life as the 'eel' lay trapped within the boat. The danger of the premature explosion of a *'Frühzünder'* torpedo was very real, and Ehlers and his torpedo men frantically cranked the tube doors further open. The torpedo eventually sprang free of confinement, and, veering erratically off course, disappeared into the darkness.

Frustrated by his inability to finish off the darkened ship, Teddy waited for the lifeboats to pull well clear before surfacing once more and calling the gun crew into action. While Waldschmidt climbed the tower as artillery officer, Webendörfer led his men on to the sodden deck casing, heavy harnesses securing them to the boat in the darkness. Within the hull, the ammunition was broken out of its store beneath the decking next to the commander's 'cabin', unloaded from each individual metal container and passed laboriously by hand through the conning tower hatch and out to the waiting gun crew. As each round slid down the small chute that folded down from the conning tower's front, it was taken and held in readiness for use by

In the early morning darkness, shells impacted the MV *Vardaas* until she eventually slipped beneath the waves (below). Haring's photograph is of dubious quality, but it nonetheless shows the flames of the impact of 8.8cm artillery fire battering the Norwegian tanker.

the two loaders on hand for the task. At 0710 hours the gun barked its first shot.

Over the next twenty-five minutes, fifty shells streaked across the narrow gap that separated the two vessels, thirty-five of them impacting on *Vardaas* in a brilliant pyrotechnic display. Amid the shooting there were several misfires, caused perhaps by split cartridge cases or defective production within the ammunition, but there were still enough hits to settle the issue of *Vardaas'* survival. The Norwegian tanker was soon burning and sinking lower into the sea, long billowing flames leaping from the holds and the combustible fumes from cargoes long past.

Finally the crescendo of cannon fire ceased. Webendörfer and his triumphant crew secured the heavy tampion on to the gun barrel and removed the delicate sighting equipment for their return below decks. The tanker continued to burn fiercely as Teddy ordered course set away from the area and out to open sea: '0750hrs. EE 9923. Shot our bolt. Head for home.'

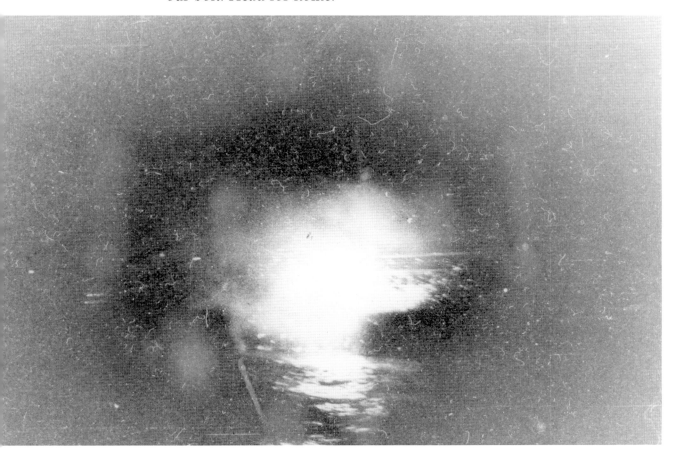

Behind them, the Norwegian continued to burn through the rest of the day, sighted by a USAAF B-18 bomber in a 'sinking condition' before she finally succumbed to the inrushing water and went under on 31 August. The forty-one shipwrecked survivors, mainly Norwegians but including one Belgian, one Australian, one Dane, two Britons and fourteen Chinese, had in the meantime landed safely in Plymouth Bay only hours after the initial attack.

As Dönitz acknowledged receipt of Suhren's message signalling the beginning of his return, BdU staff were also receiving reports from Wattenberg's *U 162* of their latest success. On 31 August Wattenberg radioed BdU to arrange a fuel transfer with any nearby U-boat, his bunkers too low to allow any margin of safety for an Atlantic crossing. Ironically, *U 564* was now in a position to be of assistance to the larger boat by transferring a small amount of diesel fuel that would be surplus to requirements for the return journey. Thus, once again, *U 564* rendezvoused with Wattenberg, this time transferring oil from the Type VII in grid square ED4963 east of St Lucia. The smaller boat's refuelling from the *Milchkuh U 463* had provided enough diesel to be able to spare two cubic metres for Wattenberg, providing a small reserve fuel level for *U 162*. The meeting was brief, perilously exposed during the fifteen-minute fuel transfer, anti-aircraft guns manned and men of both crews not needed for the fuelling standing at Battle Stations. The boats headed parallel with one another, only a dozen metres of water separating the two, hoses snaking from one to the other as the fuel was pumped aboard *U 162*. After the successful refuelling Wattenberg radioed his situation to Lorient. It was to be his last signal.

Two days later, as *U 162* lingered in the shipping lanes between Barbados and Trinidad, Wattenberg attempted to attack what he took to be a single destroyer. In fact it was trio of British destroyers— HMS *Pathfinder*, *Quentin* and *Vimy*—travelling for Trinidad and convoy duty. Wattenberg fired a single torpedo minutes after *Pathfinder* obtained ASDIC contact and changed course to intercept. The torpedo was seen, and Wattenberg was subjected to violent and accurate depth charges. With mounting damage, Wattenberg chose to escape surfaced as night fell, but *Vimy*, equipped with the new Type 271 centimetric radar, obtained a firm contact and gave chase, opening fire shortly afterwards as the sleek German boat came into view. Wattenberg tried a last desperate ruse, firing two red flares into the sky, temporarily blinding *Vimy*'s lookouts, and then swinging to port as *Vimy* attempted to ram. The two ships began a last battle of close turning circles, before Wattenberg gave in and ordered his

Bereft of ammunition, *U 564* headed home. An opportunity was taken to pass some fuel to *U 162* before departing the western Atlantic. Here (upper photograph) the two boats sail side by side as the diesel transfer begins, *U 162* to the right.

The stern 3.7cm gun on *U 162*'s deck was of little real use (lower). Holding a rate of fire too slow against enemy aircraft and a calibre too small against enemy ships, it was not often used.

boat scuttled. As his crew raced for the open deck, *Vimy* impacted upon *U 162*, her port screw smashing through the U-boat's pressure hull at the engine room. The hardened German steel proved too strong, and *Vimy*'s port propeller sheared off. While the German crew leapt from their boat, *Vimy* limped away. The British destroyer's captain was determined to ensure the demise of the now stationary U-boat and dropped a single depth charge below the sinking boat which exploded in the water and injured many of the already struggling survivors. *U 162*'s LI, *Oblt (Ing.)* Edgar Stierwald, was the last man aboard, engaged in ensuring the boat's scuttling as the depth charge exploded. He never came out, and *U 162* upended and went under. Wattenberg and forty-eight of his men were pulled from the sea, Stierwald and one other remaining unaccounted for.[2]

As Wattenberg began his last desperate battle against the British, the men of *U 564* were far out into the expansive Atlantic, already relaxing as the boat neared the boundary of the maximum range of any Allied land-based aircraft. The constant stream of radio traffic that clouded the ether was compiled and decoded by the rotating radio watches, one message received on 2 September raising

As seen from *U 564*'s conning tower, the fuel line is passed across to the Type IX U-boat (above). Dangerously exposed and unable to dive rapidly with so any men above decks, *U 564* had her refuelling completed within fifteen minutes (above right), after which she set course for France.
Teddy, Lawaetz and Gabler within the Officers' Mess aboard *U 564* (right). The bottles at right, on the small table, hold rum, 20 litres of which was taken to sea aboard the boat.

considerable interest for Elkerhausen's men. Quietly, the transcribed message was shown to Lawaetz and the other officers and logged separately from the rest, awaiting further news from Germany.

A single ship was sighted during the afternoon of 4 September, the funnels of an 'Australia type' freighter emerging above the flat horizon. However, with no torpedoes, and unsure of the vessel's defensive weaponry, Teddy wisely chose discretion rather than a potentially perilous gun attack and avoided contact with the ship, which continued on course to the west unmolested.

It was nine days after the first of the intriguing messages had been received aboard *U 564* that Teddy learned of their existence. Settling down to an afternoon rest in the small wardroom, he was alarmed at the sudden absence of sound from his diesel engines. Fearing some new problems with his precious boat, he raced for the Control Room. There he was perplexed by a sudden lack of activity within the usually businesslike nerve centre of the boat. Gabler, beaming from ear to ear, walked over to his captain and announced that the crew were going on deck to congratulate him. Puzzled at this somewhat enigmatic statement, Teddy followed Gabler outside, hoisting himself out of the conning tower hatch and finding the majority of his men already drawn up on the stern deck in three orderly ranks. While lookouts continued to scour the horizons and the sky, Teddy climbed down on to the deck. There Gabler held several decoded message slips in his hand and, with all the dignity that he could muster, proceeded to read them before the assembled crew. The various messages had been despatched from the pinnacle of the German naval hierarchy in western Europe:

In recognition of your proven heroism I grant to eighteen men of the German Armed Forces the Oak Leaves with Swords to the Knight's Cross. Adolf Hitler.

OKM to Suhren. On the conferral of the Oak Leaves with Swords, I convey to you my most heartfelt congratulation in grateful acknowledgment of the outstanding successes that you and your crew have accomplished. With comradely greetings. Your commander-in-chief, *Oberbefehlshaber der Marine* [Raeder].

Most heartfelt congratulation on the high award, *Oberbefehlshaber West* [Admiral Saalwächter].

To Suhren: Most hearty congratulations for the high award. Your proud flotilla.

The *Kriegstagebuch* was handwritten and updated by the boat's captain during the patrol. Once the boat had reached port, this log book would then be typed and prepared for presentation to BdU, as Dönitz used it to reconstruct in his mind the events of the mission, judging for himself the conduct of the boat and crew.

However, this was not the only honour that had been bestowed upon the commander, and shortly afterwards Gabler announced the second award:

To Suhren: I am delighted to be able to inform you, with my heartfelt congratulations, of your promotion to *Korvettenkapitän* in token of your exceptionally distinguished service against the enemy. *ObdM*, Raeder.

Heartfelt best wishes, *Heil und Sieg.* BdU

The double bestowal of both a promotion in rank and the second highest of all military honours was an amazing accomplishment. He was handed his jacket to put on as Nordmann, Gabler and Anderheyden affixed new 'piston rings' to his sleeves and wider oak leaves for his peaked cap, all cut from tin cans that Hausruckinger had put aside within his tiny galley. A small leather-bound book, bearing the *Wappen* of the three black cats, was under construction by the crew, each radio message meticulously recorded within its delicate pages and the book signed by every member of his crew.

Haring photographed the entire event, finally mustering as many of the crew as he could on the stern decking in order to capture the moment for posterity. Once Haring had finished, and before dismissing the men, Teddy gave his own speech for their benefit, praising their performance and reminding them that a captain was only as good as his crew. Then the diesels fired once more and *U 564* headed home.

Suhren's was not the only good news received by radio. At 0747 hours on 15 September, *Obermaschinenmaat* Fritz Hummel received his own message from both his wife and BdU: 'Our Heinz has arrived. Anni'; and 'All well and healthy. BdU'. The birth of his first son—a 'small U-boat with periscope'—was a momentous occasion for Hummel, and one that the crew marked by pasting a child's photograph, cut from the pages of a magazine, within the boat's radio log to mark the event. Sadly, Fritz Hummel would never live to see his son's first birthday as he was killed in action with *U 564* during the following year.

Once approaching the range of European aircraft, *U 564* was forced to make several crash-dives to avoid them, particularly as the boat edged into the Bay of Biscay. The final leg of their journey held the greatest peril of air attack since leaving the Caribbean, but it was with some relief that several alarm dives were found to have been caused by Focke-Wulf Fw 200 Condors flying overhead, not the RAF predators that roamed the approaches to France.

Before nearing Biscay, Suhren had ordered fresh haircuts and either shaves or trimmed beards for his crew. Contrary to the customary arrival of heavily bearded men from such a long cruise, Suhren was determined that his men would arrive in port looking spruced and healthy after their patrol.

By dusk on 18 September, *U 564* had again reached point 'Kern', radioing the flotilla headquarters and waiting for the escort ships to arrive, which they did shortly after dawn the following day. Two small *Vorpostenboote*, converted trawlers of the 7th *Vorpostenflottille*, sailed slowly into view, shepherding the larger *Sperrbrecher 6/Magdeburg*. The *Magdeburg* was quite typical of the type of ship used as *Sperrbrecher* by the *Kriegsmarine*. Built by Hamburg's Blohm & Voss yards in 1925, initially for the German-Australian Steamer Line, she had been taken over by Hamburg-Amerika Line in 1926. On 4 October she entered *Kriegsmarine* service as a *Sperrbrecher*, literally meaning 'barrier breaker'. Her 137-metre-long hull carried a formidable array of flak weaponry — two 10.5cm cannon, three 3.7cm twin flak cannon, two four-barrelled *Vierling* 2cm AA weapons and six *Raketenwerfer* anti-aircraft rocket projectors.

As far back as 1940, when the German Navy first took possession of French Atlantic ports, the British had begun to increase the tempo of their minelaying operations, initially using contact-fused mines. The advent of the *Sperrbrecher* was a rather unusual method employed to combat this menace to German shipping. These vessels were converted cargo ships designed primarily for clearing passages through minefields, though not as traditional minesweepers. The technique employed in the early stages of the war was simply to sail the ship into the suspected minefield and detonate any that lay in its path. With cargo holds filled with buoyant material (usually cork) it was reasoned that the *Sperrbrecher* would be difficult to sink, and some of the explosive impact would be absorbed. The early barrage breakers, understandably, suffered heavy casualties, and often no amount of impact-absorbing material could prevent the ship's keel from snapping in two.

As events showed aboard *U 564*, the cramped, humid interior of a submarine often played havoc with a man's physical well-being. A ritual observed by both Suhren and Gabler while within the 'Atlantic Gap' was the morning walk (above). Several lengths of the stern deck every day helped keep them fit, particularly Suhren, who suffered back pain from long stationary periods on the bridge. Moreover, the momentary ability to find solitude allowed the two men to talk without being overheard.

When safely within the 'Air Gap', and during days of clear visibility, a large portion of the off-duty crew were once again allowed above decks to benefit from the sunshine and fresh air (below) Lookouts still scrutinised the distant horizons.

With the introduction of magnetic and acoustic mines, new techniques were required, although the *Sperrbrecher* remained at the heart of U-boat escort duties. Coupled with their minesweeping tasks, the *Sperrbrecher* were found by the pilots of the Allied Strike Wings that operated against enemy shipping to be tough nuts to crack, the RAF term for them being 'heavy flak ships'.

The escort ships had arrived not only for Suhren's boat. As *U 564* fell into line behind them, flotilla-mate *U 203* joined the small convoy that approached the granite cliffs of the Breton coast. Unlike their last meeting, however, it was a subdued boat cutting her patrol short that ran into view behind *U 564*: Rolf Mützelburg had made one last, fatal, head-first dive from the conning tower of his boat a week previously, and *U 203* was being brought home by the IWO, *ObltzS* Hans Seidel. Sadly, Suhren's warning to Mützelburg during their July meeting within the Atlantic had ultimately proved to be correct.

Mützelburg had returned from that patrol to Brest and a triumphant reception, and was flown shortly afterwards to Berlin with 'Adi' Schnee to received the Oak Leaves in person from Adolf Hitler in the Reich Chancellery. After their joint cere-

The reason for allowing the crew above decks only in areas of relative security is obvious from these three photographs (left). In the event of a crash-dive, each of these men would have to reach the single conning tower hatch and, one by one, drop inside. The extra time that this would entail before submergence could spell disaster during an air attack. There was little formality between ranks aboard a U-boat, particularly when the crew were not on duty. Shown gathered on the *'Wintergarten'* to enjoy the sunshine are a cross-section of the boat's *Maate* and *Matrosen*. Personal hygiene was difficult at best aboard a combat boat, even when she was able to surface and the crew could come above decks (right, upper). Lice were often a problem, and could race through the confined crew if unchecked. Any area of body hair could harbour the irritating creatures, and the problem was exacerbated by the irritation caused by the tropical temperatures. Removal of the offending hair with scissors was one solution to the predicament.

Despite the relaxed atmosphere of a boat returning without ammunition and within the 'Air Gap', vigilance remained crucial to survival (right, lower).

mony, Dönitz exercised his standard procedure of offering staff positions to both men. By rotating highly decorated officers to staff or training duties, new recruits could benefit from their front-line experience. As well as that obvious reason, the possibility of another severe blow to morale in the event of the hero being sunk, such as had happened following the grievous losses of Prien, Schepke and Kretschmer during 1941 — still felt keenly the following year within the *Kriegsmarine* and German people as a whole — was averted. However, as much as he attempted to persuade his captains, cajoling them to bend to his will, the choice ultimately remained in the hands of the commander himself. While Schnee accepted the offer to join the BdU staff, Mützelburg did not want to leave *U 203* and elected to remain on board for at least one more cruise.

On 27 August *U 203* had sailed once more, bound for the western Atlantic. Fifteen days later, during a swimming break beyond the range of aircraft south-west of the Azores, Mützelburg had dived head-first from the conning tower. At the moment he sprang into the air the U-boat rolled in a long lazy swell and he struck the saddle tank with his head and shoulder. Dragged back aboard in agony, he was taken below, where he died of his injuries early the next day, 12 September 1942. The doctor aboard *U 462* examined the body before Mützelburg was confined to the deep in a formal burial at sea.

Although most aboard *U 564* mourned the loss of the ebullient Mützelburg, death at sea had become a common denominator amongst the entire U-boat service. As with most fighting men, the celebration of life became all-important, and Suhren's conning tower became crowded with men eager for a glimpse of the French landscape. Tightly coiled victory pennants, painstakingly hand-painted during the boredom of the return journey, were attached to the head of the retracted attack periscope, waiting for the grand unfurling. Atop the tube were also two crossed swords, made within the workshop ,that graced the forward end of the diesel room and designed to celebrate Suhren's award.

Beneath a brilliant blue sky, the convoy headed east towards Brest. Passing the barren outcrops that constituted the Ouessant Isles, eventually the abandoned ruins of the monastery at Pointe St-Mathieu became visible, the incongruous modern lighthouse, now a German observation and navigation station, standing immediately to seaward of it. As the Rade de Brest enveloped *U 564* within its beautiful rocky coastline, the periscope was extended

and nine victory pennants fluttered proudly above the heads of the victorious crew. Lining both edges of the entrance channel to Brest lay heavy concrete bunkers, containing the large-calibre weapons of the *Kriegsmarine*'s coastal artillery, their crews emerging to wave to the small group of vessels welcoming the U-boat crew home. The curious mixture of medieval, Napoleonic and German fortresses lay at either flank of *U 564* as she entered the Goulet de Brest, the slim channel that provided such excellent shelter and easily protected access to Brest's military harbour. More squat concrete shelters housed torpedo tubes that guarded the narrowest point of the Goulet, vessels being obliged to travel along two distinct marked channels

Obersteuermann Karl Limburg and *Bootsmannmaat* Karl-Ernst Thiel 'shoot the sun' to obtain a navigational fix (top).
During the return voyage, Suhren authorised the boat to stop for a practice target shoot, in which much of the stored flak ammunition was used. Here (above) Teddy himself mans the 2cm cannon, Wagner and Kalbach acting as loaders.

separated by the jagged edges of Toulbroch Reef that had claimed the lives of careless mariners for as long as the port had existed.

A small launch approached *U 564,* and several fellow-officers of the 1st U-Flotilla came aboard the boat, accompanied by Dr Richter, the flotilla's surgeon. The state of Suhren's men after seventy days at sea impressed Richter. They had lost little weight and appeared groomed and healthy to his brief spot checks. But the effect of so long a period at sea was lingering with Suhren:

> I myself felt in some way a different person. The officers standing around me seemed more distant, their laughter,more remote. But there was no reason why it should have been different. After previous patrols I hadn't felt the same way, this sensation of 'being apart'. Perhaps the stress of all those weeks of being responsible for them hadn't worn off yet. But the feeling of being isolated didn't go away.[3]

Perchance it was the result of his longest war patrol that endured within the young commander as his boat approached harbour and

safety, or maybe it was the knowledge that this was his last combat patrol and he had survived, the nearby *U 203* a sure reminder of the many friends who had not. Nonetheless, Suhren's daze and distance gradually evaporated with the approaching spectacle of Brest before him. The ancient château that crowned the waterfront to starboard, the magnificent Naval Academy flotilla headquarters and the imposing concrete U-boat bunkers created an indelible image of Brest at war as an occupied city. The broad medieval streets that arced over the city's hilltop held a multitude of Frenchmen and Germans alike as *U 564* approached the waterfront docks that vividly showed the ravages of Allied aerial bombardment that had hit its stride in 1941 when three German capital ships had been moored in the harbour or ensconced in drydock. The 1st U-Flotilla's adjutant delayed *U 564* from entering the basin of the military harbour until

Oberbootsmannmaat Heinrich Bartels takes his turn to shoot (left and below). Suhren had once complained in person to Hitler that the flak weapon was prone to rusting on operational voyages, despite constant attention from its crew. However, despite Hitler's instant demands to Armaments Minister Albert Speer for the problem to be addressed, it was never fully solved.

the waiting reception ceremony had been completely organised, allowing Suhren to enter the walled enclave only once things were in order.

U 564 switched over to silent electric motors and eased gracefully towards the pier head opposite the gaping bunker entrance. However, even the simple act of ending his patrol resulted in one of the most memorable displays of Suhren's sense of humour. Beneath the gaze of a huge assembly of Navy and Army officers, Brest's mayor and mayoress and a naval guard of honour, *U 564* approached the pier. Within the crush of excited people, Suhren's keen eyes spotted his good friend Horst 'Hein' Uphoff, commander of *U 84* and fellow-cadet from the Crew of 35. Uphoff, as renowned as Suhren for his free spirit as well as the many ribald political jokes he would recite at the expense of various Nazi Party members, had recently arrived from his own patrol within the Gulf of Mexico,

The health and appearance of himself and his crew remained constantly at the forefront of Suhren's thinking during his final war patrol. He wished to arrive at Brest looking fresh and clean despite two months at sea. As *U 564* crossed the mid-Atlantic, Richard Steinert gave Teddy's hair a final trim (right). (Below) Still safe from the threat of aircraft, Lawaetz (left of picture) and Suhren enjoy slumbering *al fresco*.

After weeks at sea, maintenance continued to remain of paramount importance. A loose deck plate on *U 564*'s *Wintergarten* caused problems (below right), not only because of the noise generated during underwater travel but also because the air intake for the diesel room was immediately below.

Maintenance continues (left) on the loose loose deck plate on *U 564*'s *'Wintergarten'*.

On 1 September 1942, all available
crew were drawn up on the stern
deck for the surprise announcement
of Teddy's award of the Swords to
his Knight's Cross and Oak Leaves,
as well as his promotion to
Korvettenkapitän.

Teddy always took a personal
interest in such areas of maintenance. Here (far left), roused
from his bunk and still clad in
pyjamas, he assists his men in
rectifying the fault.
If all else fails, use the hammer! In
this photograph (left), another
distinctive identifying feature of
Teddy Suhren's is visible: on his left
hand is a small ruby ring, an
heirloom that had been within the
Suhren family for 300 years by the
time it came to Teddy.

reaching Brest five days previously. The effects of both the increasing pressure of improving American defences and the celebrations at survival that had stretched on for days following his return had left their mark on Uphoff, and he appeared tired and drawn to Teddy's eyes.

Acting with more spontaneity than careful deliberation, Teddy bellowed across the narrowing gulf of water by megaphone: 'Well

(Left, top) 'In recognition of your proven heroism I grant to eighteen men of the German Armed Forces the Oak Leaves with Swords to the Knight's Cross. Adolf Hitler.' . . . 'To Suhren: I am delighted to be able to inform you, with my heartfelt congratulations, of your promotion to *Korvettenkapitän* in token of your exceptionally distinguished service against the enemy. ObdM, Raeder.' Promotion to *Korvettenkapitän* required new rank insignia (left and above), and thus Gabler, Nordmann and Anderheyden attached the three broad 'piston rings' to Teddy's jacket and wider oak leaves to the brim of his cap, all cut from tin cans hoarded within Hausruck-inger's galley.

Hein, are the Nazis still at the helm?' Faces blanched and most of the assembled crowd looked uncomfortably at each other before murmurs of assent drifted back to *U 564*. Upon hearing that they were, Teddy promptly shouted for both engines full astern and backed *U 564* towards open sea again, much to the quiet amusement and embarrassed glances of his waiting friends.

As the way came off his boat and Teddy's men threw their heavy mooring lines to the waiting hands ashore, *U 564* came to rest against the hull of a derelict barge that acted as floating pontoon within the tidal basin. Alongside the naval personnel and French and German dignitaries were several Army officers, recently returned from Russia for a period of recuperation in the backwater of Brittany. Unfortunately, in their enthusiasm to get closer to the U-boat, several of them walked from the jetty on to the barge's makeshift roof, collapsing it and causing several serious injuries.

As Suhren later ruefully remarked once the ambulances had taken the hapless Army officers away, 'Even in port, *U 564* did pretty well for excitement!'

The twin recognition of promotion and the award of Germany's second highest decoration for valour had truly elevated Teddy Suhren to the pantheon of the élite: only four other men within the U-boat service received the Crossed Swords to their Knight's Cross and Oak Leaves. However, Teddy was keenly aware that his crew had played an enormous role in his own combat record, and, never one to ignore his men, he spent several minutes speaking to them of their part in his own personal rewards.

Once the speech was over, the time came for Haring to record the event for posterity. In the photograph below right he can be seen using a small cine camera to film part of the crew; Teddy looks on.

The first of several posed crew shots taken by Haring is shown below left. However, Teddy considered that not enough of his men were featured in the first series of photographs and eventually all but an absolute skeleton crew were assembled on the stern deck to record the momentous occasion (below right).

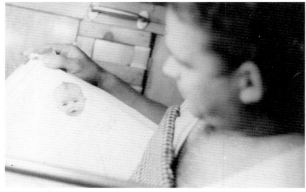

(Above) At 0747 hours on 15 September, *Obermaschinenmaat* Fritz Hummel received a message transmitted from BdU—the arrival of 'one small U-boat with periscope'. The birth of Hummel's first son was marked by *U 564*'s entire crew, Haring pasting a child's photograph, cut from the pages of a magazine, within the boat's radio log next to the recorded entry of Dönitz's message. Here Hummel (in his bunk), Willi Anderheyden and Heinz Webendörfer read the brief congratulatory message. Hummel would see his infant son three times over the next eleven months: he was among the twenty-eight men killed on *U 564* when she was sunk in June 1943. The other two petty officers are wearing heavy rain gear, although Anderheyden, as part of the boat's Technical Branch, would not have had to stand watch outside. Dönitz was acutely aware of the positive effect that such personal messages had on his men, and Hummel's notification was transmitted at the same time as similar news for three other men aboard different U-boats.

Finally, on 19 September—the day after *U 564* arrived at Point Kern—the U-boat rendezvoused with its *Vorpostenboot* escort. Under the flak and minesweeping protection of the escort ships, Teddy allowed men once again on to the conning tower after general confinement below decks as the boat crossed the increasingly dangerous Bay of Biscay.

(Right) The small converted trawlers of Brest's 7th *Vorpostenflotilla* bore the brunt of escort duties for incoming and outgoing U-boats. Robust and seaworthy, the trawlers were in constant danger from air attack, and their elimination was soon placed at a priority among the tasks of the RAF as a means to disrupt U-boat sailings. In the foreground here can be seen the crossed swords constructed in *U 564*'s workshop and affixed to the attack periscope to celebrate Teddy's award. The boat's commissioning pennant is already streaming from the small commanders flagpole—a tradition for returning boats.

The smaller trawlers were soon joined by the larger converted merchant *Sperrbrecher 6/Magdeburg*, identifiable by her distinctive high smokestack (right, lower). *Magdeburg* had been in service with the Hamburg-Amerika Line before being requisitioned for *Kriegsmarine* service. Sporting a formidable array of flak weapons, *Sperrbrecher* were mine clearance vessels in whose wake U-boats would sail to and from port. Here, as his crew study the distant *Magdeburg*, the previously prepared string of *'Erfolgswimpeln'* (success pennants) has been attached to the retracted periscope, preparing to unfurl as the coast draws into view.

(Left) Communications man Ewald Gaiser signals by flag semaphore to the *Sperrbrecher* escort and then by lamp to *U 203*, trailing behind Suhren's boat. It was a subdued crew aboard their flotilla-mate, one week after the death of their popular commander Mützelburg. With the entire crew looking fit, washed and groomed Teddy prepared to enter port. Here (below left) the boat's three senior non-commissioned officers have prepared for their return. From the left, *Obermaschinisten* Mattern and Kräh and *Bootsmann* Webendörfer enjoy their final run in to port. *Obermaschinist* Heinz Mattern stands before *U 564*'s deck gun (below right). Like many of the more experienced crew aboard the boat, Mattern was due to leave *U 564*, scheduled to begin training as a Chief Engineer at the end of this voyage.

IIWO Herbert Waldschmidt, obviously pleased to be nearing home (right). Waldschmidt sailed once more aboard *U 564* before beginning his own commander's course.

As the Breton coastline looms into view (far right), the other 'passenger' aboard *U 564* poses for a photograph by Haring. *Leutnant* (*Ing.*) Eberhard Hammermüller learned much from his time as part of Gabler's technical crew, taking the experience with him when posted as Chief Engineer on *U 921* in May 1943. He died aboard the latter boat during her third patrol when she was sunk with all hands on 30 September 1944.

U 564's petty officers prepare for landfall (below left). From the left are Joseph Harsch, Willi Ander-heyden, Gerhard Ehlers, Heinz Nordmann and Heinrich Bartels. All but two of these men would survive the war.

Enlisted men also crowd atop the conning tower as *U 564* nears Brest (below, far right). From the left are Richard Steinert, Heinrich Wagner, Heinz Schmutzler, Walter Labahn, Helmut Brock and Wilhelm Bigge.

As *U 564* approached the Goulet de Brest in the *Sperrbrecher*'s wake, the success pennants (*'Erfolgswimpeln '*) were finally unfurled (above), nine streaming from the attack periscope as the U-boat passed beneath the guns of naval artillery batteries on either side of the entrance channel.

Once the inspections were over the crew relaxed, eating seasonal strawberries brought aboard by nurses from Brest's naval hospital (right). Ewald Gaiser and Eduard Kalbach are enjoying the fresh fruit. Over Kalbach's shoulder, the gaping mouth of a pen of Brest's formidable U-boat bunker can just be discerned.

Epilogue

TEDDY'S return sparked much celebration within the Naval Academy headquarters of the 1st U-Flotilla. Recently decorated and promoted, he marched at the head of his crew from the bunkers to the Academy, where the pressure of command gradually began to dissipate. A banquet within the building had been organised, and the entire crew began their duty of rejoicing at their success and survival. The days passed slowly as the men unwound, half of them soon to receive home leave, later rotating with those who had remained in Brest.

Among the decorations awarded to Teddy's crew members after their voyage was a German Cross in Gold for *Oblt (Ing.)* Ulrich Gabler. Teddy had requested a Knight's Cross, but the decoration had been amended by those above him, for reasons unspecified. This patrol marked the end of both Gabler's and Suhren's operational careers. Gabler was transferred to Germany, where he began work within the U-boat design teams, concentrating initially on the *Schnorchel*, soon to be vitally important to the U-boat Service. He entered the central U-boat Design Office of Glückauf in Blankenburg/Harz, and quickly rose to become the departmental director. Gabler ended the war working on the 'Walter boat', having been brought on board the project in early 1943 on the recommendation of another ex-U-boat LI, Heinrich Heep of *U 203,* who had been seconded to the design department in October 1942.[1] Meanwhile Suhren left command of *U 564* and the ranks of 1st U-Flotilla for a position as instructor at the 22nd U-Flotilla (2nd U-Boat Training Division, or 2 ULD) with his friend Erich Topp.

Teddy's final post-patrol debriefing by Dönitz ended with a gentle but firm rebuke. He was regaling his Commander-in-Chief with the story of Limburg's remark that the U-boat's interior had been as 'dark as a bear's arse' during their diesel fire, when Dönitz cut him short. Suhren had already earned his commander's displeasure years before as a young *Leutnant* aboard *U 48* by swearing during gunnery drill. Using his sternest voice, 'The Lion' reminded him that he was a prominent figure, highly decorated and respected within the

The reception given to Teddy and his crew was ecstatic—although turbulent to begin with! Once moored alongside the sea wall that fringed the military harbour, flotilla commander *KK* Werner Winter strode aboard *U 564* and inspected the immaculately turned-out crew.

Within the Naval Academy Headquarters of the 1st U-Flotilla, a ceremonial banquet was held for the returned crew. Winter removed his *Korvettenkapitän*'s cap and allowed Teddy to try it on for size. To the right is *Kaptlt* Walter Schug, commander of *U 86*, which had also returned that day from the Atlantic. *U 86* had made a single small sinking during its two months at sea. The mural in the background depicts the imposing red brick structure of the Naval Memorial in Laboe, near Kiel.

Wehrmacht, and that he should think before opening his mouth—and definitely choose his language with great care.

Dönitz's assessment of Teddy's final combat patrol was summed up in two sentences appended to the official typed version of the boat's War Diary that would remain in BdU records: 'Excellent undertaking by this proven commander. The convoy attacks, both in conception and execution, were carried out in an exemplary manner.'[2]

Teddy's crew, who had come to have complete and unswerving trust in their captain, lamented his departure from Brest. One at a time, he said goodbye to the men that had served beneath him, many since *U 564* had been commissioned. Several of the boat's 'old guard'

were also moving on, either to fresh operational postings or to training positions within the *Kriegsmarine*. Among those who bade farewell were *Obermaschinisten* Kräh and Mattern, as well as Karl Limburg, who was promoted and posted to the 23rd and later 26th U-Training Flotillas. Ulf Lawaetz would sail once again as IWO on *U 564*, beneath new commander *ObltzS* Hans Fiedler, before he undertook commander training and assumed control of a newly built *U 672* within the Howaldts Werke dockyard in Hamburg during April 1943. Four patrols as part of the 6th U-Flotilla saw Lawaetz make no sinkings, his final voyage ending on 18 July 1944 when *U 672* was depth-charged and forced to the surface in the English Channel. There, amidst thick banks of fog, he and his crew ensured that the boat would scuttle, and then abandoned ship. Clinging together, they were eventually picked up by Allied air–sea

rescue forces as the fog dissipated, and they spent the remainder of the war as prisoners.

Up until the day he died in 2001, Lawaetz continued to be plagued by nightmares of his sinking, although he tried to put the memories of the war behind him. Following his release from prison in December 1945, he travelled to Bünde, the centre of Germany's cigar industry. Initially working as an interpreter, he eventually rose to the top as manager of a cigar factory.

Herbert Waldschmidt also sailed under Fiedler, leaving the boat in April 1943 to undergo commander training. He captained the training boat *U 146* and later became the 'commander in waiting' for two Type XXI U-boats, *U 2374* and *U 4719*, although both were damaged by bombing and neither was put into service before the war's end. He finally commanded an operational Type XXI when, as a *Fregattenkapitän* within the *Bundesmarine*, he skippered the salvaged *U 2540*, renamed *Wilhelm Bauer* and now on display at Bremerhaven's Nautical Museum after being retired from years of active service and reconfigured to resemble its wartime state.

The last of *U 564*'s officers from their summer patrol of 1942, *Leutnant (Ing.)* Eberhard Hammermüller, benefited from his experience aboard as a part of Gabler's technical crew and was transferred to become chief engineer on *U 921* when she entered service in May 1943. He died with all other fifty hands when their boat was sunk within the Arctic south-west of Bear Island by a Swordfish aircraft escorting convoy RA.60 on 30 September 1944.

Teddy Suhren travelled on to Berlin after his debriefing by Dönitz. There, he once again found himself surrounded by the nation's élite, beginning with breakfast with the usually stern Erich Raeder:

> This time I came up to Berlin on the overnight train. In the proper manner as befits a soldier, I appeared at 1355 hours in the Kaiserhof. There I met the *Oberbefehlshaber der Marine* already there and said, apologetically so to speak, 'Oh *Großadmiral*, are you here already?' Whereupon he replied with a laugh, 'Yes, yes, and you without a trail of exhaust fumes today!'[3]

After a brief visit to see Hitler to receive his official decoration of the Swords to his Knight's Cross, Teddy found himself invited by Martin Bormann to the Obersalzburg, the

Ulf Lawaetz sailed once again as IWO on *U 564* before undergoing captain's training and taking command of *U 672* during April 1943. Here he is pictured at the end of one of his four patrols as part of the 6th U-Flotilla. Lawaetz's combat career ended on 18 July 1944 when *U 672* was depth charged and forced to the surface in the English Channel. Having managed to save his entire crew and scuttling his boat, Lawaetz, and his men, spent the remainder of the war as prisoners.

private retreat of the *Führer* and his closest associates near Berchtesgaden, where Erich Topp was already a guest. Suhren mingled with those who occupied the dizzy heights of power within the Third Reich, 'boogying' with Eva Braun and her sister, despite the wartime ban on dancing, and staying as a guest with an uncharacteristically approachable and seemingly relaxed Bormann and his family.

Even after Teddy's departure from Brest, his shadow loomed large over the port city. Claus-Peter Carlsen still laughingly remembers, sixty years after the end of the war, the many times that he was entertained with tales of Suhren's exploits after his own arrival at the 1st U-Flotilla base in October 1942 as *Oberleutnant zur See* commander of *U 732*: 'Teddy Suhren, well . . . he was a beast! . . . Werner Winter, he was the commander of Teddy Suhren and Uphoff, both of these crazy bastards, and he told all kinds of stories about these two.'[4]

Indeed, the legends of Teddy's disrespect for authority and prowess at the bar even made it as far as the US Navy, where his name cropped up prominently during an interrogation of *U 521*'s captured commander *Kapitänleutnant* Klaus Bargsten:

Ulrich Gabler's impressive combat record earned him a German Cross in Gold, which was awarded in Brest on 15 October 1942. It was the end of his combat career as he was transferred to become part of Germany's U-boat design teams.

> [Bargsten's] most intimate friend and classmate was KK Reinhard 'Teddy' Suhren. It was stated that Suhren, good looking and popular, could considerably lower the alcoholic stocks of any port in which he found himself . . . On another occasion Suhren was stalking a convoy which he had previously reported . . . In due course he received an 'inspirational' message from Dönitz telling him to 'pursue relentlessly and attack fiercely'. Upon returning from this cruise, which was highly successful, Suhren was summoned to Dönitz's office to give his report.
>
> In the course of the interview, Suhren violated decorum by referring to the signal as unnecessary, if not insulting. Dönitz was momentarily taken aback by this impudence, but recovered in time to seize Suhren by the neck, lay him across a table, and administer a sound spanking to the naughty boy.[5]

Even so, Suhren rose meteorically through the ranks. Later, in May 1944, he became commander of all U-boats stationed in Norway, *FdU Norwegen* (later *FdU Nordmeer*), exercising operational control of Arctic U-boats. Shortly afterwards he received his final promotion to *Fregattenkapitän*. By then, his only combat command had gone. On 14 June 1943 *U 564* was classified as *Vermißt zwei Stern* — 'missing two stars', *Kriegsmarine* parlance for 'confirmed lost'. 'The boat departed Bordeaux 9 June. During 14 June it was attacked and sunk by enemy aircraft in (Grid Reference) Bruno Fritz 7549. Twenty-eight sailors dead. Eighteen, plus the commander, rescued.'[6]

Fiedler's veteran *U 564* was one of five U-boats crossing the Bay of Biscay, surfaced in accordance with a new BdU directive that boats stand and fight if attacked by aircraft. She was bombed first by a No 228 RAF Squadron Sunderland and heavily damaged, rendered unable to dive. The 10th U-Flotilla's *U 185* was instructed to escort *U 564* south to the Spanish coast, where Fiedler could attempt repairs. *Z 24* and *Z 32* of Bordeaux's 8th Destroyer Flotilla prepared to sail and rendezvous with the two U-boats.

However, by unhappy coincidence, the following day marked the opening of a new RAF anti-submarine air campaign centring on Biscay and named 'Musketry'. During 14 June the two slow-moving U-boats inched painfully towards neutral Spain when a Whitley of No 10 Operational Training Unit, sighted them 90 miles north-west of Ferrol. The bomber began circling as both *U 564* and *U 185* opened fire with all flak weapons. Two hours later a Hampden of No 415 Squadron also arrived, and the Whitley, piloted by Flight Sergeant, A. J. Benson, opened its attack. Spraying the U-boats with machine-gun fire, Benson roared overhead and straddled *U 564* with six depth charges, ripping open the hull and breaking the U-boat's spine. Benson also suffered during the attack, and with damage to his aircraft's hydraulics and starboard engine, he was forced to put down into the sea 80 miles south-west of the Scillies.[7]

Maus, aboard *U 185*, briefly and unsuccessfully attempted to attach a towline to the ailing *U 564*, but the latter was gradually swamped and went to the bottom. Only Fiedler and seventeen men were rescued, the remainder accompanying *U 564* on her final dive. The boat's entire technical and radio crew were killed, either by the initial blasts or in trying to stop their battered U-boat from flooding. In fact, the horrific mortality rate of Germany's Second World War U-boat service can be amply demonstrated by the fact that none of the other U-boats pictured within the photographs of Suhren's final patrol survived the war: *U 154*, *U 203*, *U 463* and *U 654* were all sunk in action, while *U 129* was scuttled and blown up within the Kéroman bunkers at Lorient, crippled by worn-out batteries. Even the heavily armed *Sperrbrecher Magdeburg*, photographed by Haring leading *U 564* into port, was destroyed by RAF fighter bombers in 1944, and virtually the entire 7th Flotilla of smaller *Vorpostenboot* escorts was also blasted into oblivion by the overwhelming Allied air and naval power that soon hemmed in the French Atlantic bases.

Less than two years after the destruction of *U 564*, the war was at last over. Suhren ended his naval career as *FdU Nord*, a prisoner of the British in Oslo during 1945. He was held for a year in Oslo's

Teddy, pictured here with Adalbert 'Adi' Schnee (left) and Hellmut Ebell, became commander of all northern Norwegian-based U-boats in May 1944, as FdU Nord. He ended the war as a *Fregatten-kapitän* and a prisoner of the British, after having exercised operational control of Arctic U-boats for a year.

Achenschloss prison, where he was reunited with his erstwhile commander Hans Rudolf Rösing.[8] It was while a prisoner that Teddy learnt of the death of his parents and sister. Living in Sudetenland during the final days of the war, they had been surrounded by 'partisans' as German forces withdrew and the Czech uprising began. Geert Suhren killed his wife and daughter rather than let them fall into the hands of the mob, and then he killed himself.

On 12 April 1946 Teddy was released. He travelled home to a defeated Germany. He spent some time on an estate at Kleverhof near Bad Schwartau, where the large property had been divided up, Teddy gaining sixteen acres of land. Out of the meagre savings from his service pay, he bought himself a small caravan and a cow and re-established contact with his wife Jutta, the daughter of a *Luftwaffe* staff officer whom he had married in 1943. Teddy found her and their daughter Beatrix in Allgaü, where she was a waitress in an American Officers' Mess. Much to Teddy's shock and dismay, she had in the meantime acquired an American boyfriend, and their already shaky marriage disintegrated completely.

In low spirits, Teddy returned to Kleverhof, where he experienced yet another setback. The local populace had not reckoned on his returning, and had divided up his small parcel of land amongst them. Despondent, but unwilling to give up, Suhren then departed for Kiel, where he sold a silver-fox fur coat that had belonged to his wife and so acquired his soon-to-be infamous 'Schnapps Factory' in a garden shed on the edge of the shattered town. There Teddy distilled 38 per cent proof black rum from sugar—his so-called 'torpedo spirit'. In 1946 schnapps was more valuable than Reichsmark notes, and Teddy's new business flourished as he also began to butcher local meat for the black market. However, before long the local police were tipped off about Teddy's enterprise, and shortly before they arrived to break up his operation Suhren destroyed his still and took himself back to the estate in Schwartau, where his caravan was still standing. There he earned a small wage by helping farmers with part-time sheep-shearing.

During the summer of 1947, his brother Gerd, working for the post-war German Minesweeping Administration and still maintaining close contacts within Germany's maritime community, finally found Teddy a job more suited to his considerable talents. His task was to revive Germany's decrepit merchant-shipping oil industry for an international mineral-oil concern. Buying himself a BMW 350 for 850 Reichsmarks, Teddy rattled off to Hamburg and eventually became the manager of the mineral oil business based in the city.

Although relations with his former wife had become amicable once more, he soon married again, to Hannelore, and lived initially in Bad Dietzenbach (Hessen) and later Hamburg. They eventually had three daughters, Katrin, Gesa and Mara joining their half-sister Beatrix from Teddy's first marriage, and Teddy's life was finally once again stabilised and comfortable. He refused to enlist in the *Bundes-marine* despite many offers, stating that he could not serve in the Navy where the wartime soldiers were looked down upon as criminals. However, he was a founder of the German Naval Association (DMB), and was appointed Founding Chairman on 31 May 1953 at a meeting in Wilhelmshaven. There he spoke before 20,000 former fellow naval veterans in the town square. On 15 May 1954 he also made a key address to U-boat veterans at the first national *U-Boot Fahrer* meeting in Hamburg. As he remembered the many men who had lost their lives during five years of war, he also spoke passionately about reconciliation of the warring nations and the injustice of both Dönitz and Erich Raeder being incarcerated in Spandau Prison as war criminals.

Reinhard 'Teddy' Suhren died on 25 January 1984 in Hamburg. It was only immediately before his death that he informed people that he had been suffering from painful terminal cancer of the stomach for some time. Teddy had given up smoking some years earlier, after his doctor had become concerned about his health, informing him that either smoking or drinking had to go. He chose the former, but eventually succumbed to cancer nonetheless.

Many attended his funeral to mourn the loss of such a remarkable man, among them Erich Topp, who later wrote within the pages of his autobiography of his own emotions during the brief funeral service:

> I recognized many of the faces around me: Godt, Kretschmer, Korth, Bargsten, Cremer and others — after all those years they looked somewhat strange to me. The Knight's Crosses on their grey suits did not quite seem to befit the occasion.
>
> At last the gates to Hall B open. We barely hear organ music playing in the background, not live but from a record. I sit down in the third row. The coffin is surrounded by wreaths and flowers and flanked by an honour guard of

Bundesmarine officers. The music stops. The representative of Teddy's graduating class, Crew 35, is the first to speak. After a brief, indefinable organ interlude he is followed by the honorary president of the Naval Association, whose address seems lively and loud. Then it is the turn of the submarine commander under whom Teddy served as executive officer [Herbert Schultze]. He speaks hesitatingly, searching for words, visibly moved. Finally, the spokesman for the Association of Submariners. Using the famous lines of the Flanders Flotilla of World War I, he suggests that, on account of Teddy's usually unkempt appearance and overall bad deeds, St. Peter would likely send him to a special heaven for U-boat commanders, where they can continue their old ways of singing, drinking, and merrymaking.

For all who spoke, Teddy seemed to be representing the stereotypical *Landsknecht,* the soldier of fortune of bygone days who made merry with his friends as their drinking buddy, whose sense of humour was legendary, and who did not always stop at the limits of the possible.

The picture I had of Teddy was quite different. To me he was a friend with whom I had gone through this damned war, a man marked by the terrible fate of his family. I saw his exaggerated honesty as something designed to hide his true feelings. I listened to his colourful humour, but it too only masked the cynicism of a lost existence, the endorsement of unpopular views.

The words that filled the room failed to reach me. A trumpeter played *Das Lied von guten Kameraden.* When it was over, the curtain came down after this last act in the dramatic life of my friend Reinhard Suhren. We mourners left Hall B through the crowd that was already waiting outside for the next funeral. Teddy's relatives left in a car that had been standing by with its engine running. I could not even express my condolences to them. I was told there was to be a get-together of the old-timers. I was too disappointed, too depressed, to participate. Ali Cremer took me back to the station.[9]

Thus, thirty-one years after *U 564* had gone to the seabed with twenty-eight crewmen entombed within her, another man was laid to rest in the exact location that *U 564* and the 'Three Black Cats' went down. On 25 October 1984 *Kapitän* Temeier, master of the 5,084-ton freighter MV *Papua*, ordered all available crew on deck at 1600 hours for a brief ceremony as the ship lay at 46° 30′ N, 07° 18′ W. There, in accordance with his last wishes, the ashes of Reinhard 'Teddy' Suhren were scattered on the gentle Atlantic swell, reunited with the boat that he had made famous.

Reinhard 'Teddy' Suhren
Fregattenkapitän
Knight's Cross with Oak Leaves and Swords.
1916–1984

☰ Appendices

APPENDIX ONE: THE CREW OF *U 564*

Note: This list gives names of crew members during U 564*'s longest war patrol, July–September 1942. An asterisk denotes a crew member who was killed in action during the Second World War, together with the boat in which he lost his life.*

Seaman's Branch

Reinhard 'Teddy' Suhren	*Kapitänleutnant/ Korvettenkapitän*	Captain
Ulf Lawaetz	*Oberleutnant zur See*	IWO
Herbert Waldschmidt	*Leutnant zur See*	IIWO
Karl 'Stürkorl' Limburg	*Stabsobersteuermann*	IIIWO and Navigator
Heinz Webendörfer	*Oberbootsmann*	Crew Chief/Artillery (Seaman1)
Heinrich Bartels	*Bootsmann*	Ammunition Chief (Seaman 2) (*U 867)
Karl-Ernst Thiel	*Bootsmannsmaat*	Artillery/Personnel Admin. (Seaman 3)
Rudi Elkerhausen	*Oberfunkmaat*	Senior Radio Petty Officer (*U 564)
Willi Anderheyden	*Oberfunkmaat*	Second Radio Petty Officer
Gerhard Ehlers	*Obermechanikermaat*	Torpedo Mate
Werner Grünert	*Matrosenobergefreiter*	Combat helmsman
Heinz Schmutzler	*Matrosengefreiter*	Seaman/Stern hydroplanes/ 2cm Flak
Heinrich Wagner	*Matrosengefreiter*	Seaman/Helm/2cm Flak
Roland Schiedhelm	*Matrosenobergefreiter*	Seaman/Artillery (*U 333)
Ernst Schlittenhard	*Matrosenobergefreiter*	Seaman/Artillery
Eduard Kalbach	*Matrosengefreiter*	Seaman/Artillery
Richard Steinert	*Matrosengefreiter*	Seaman/Artillery (*U 564)
Paul Stephan	*Matrosengefreiter*	Seaman/Artillery (*U 564)
Herman Hausruckinger	*Matrosengefreiter*	Cook
Horst Becker	*Mechanikerober- gefreiter*	Torpedo Mechanic
Wilhelm Bigge	*Mechanikerober- gefreiter*	Torpedo Mechanic (*U 333)
Werner Apitz	*Funkobergefreiter*	Radio/Hydrophone (*U 564)
Ewald Gaiser	*Funkobergefreiter*	Radio/Hydrophone (*U 1222)
Meimes Haring	*Propaganda Kompanie Maat*	War Correspondent

Technical Branch

Ulrich Gabler	*Oberleutnant (Ingenieur)*	Chief Engineer
Eberhard Hammermüller	*Leutnant (Ingenieur) der Reserve*	Trainee Chief Engineer (*U 921)
Hermann Kräh	*Obermaschinist*	Diesel Chief
Heinz Mattern	*Obermaschinist*	Electric Motor Chief
Emil Grade	*Maschinenobermaat*	Control Room Mate
Franz Stocker	*Obermaschinenmaat*	Starboard Diesel Engineer (*U 1024)
Fritz Hummel	*Obermaschinenmaat*	Port Diesel Engineer (*U 564)
Johannes Neumann	*Maschinenobermaat*	Starboard Electric Engineer (*U 722)
Heinz Nordmann	*Maschinenobermaat*	Port Electric Engineer
Joseph Harsch	*Maschinenobermaat*	Electric Motor Mate (*U 564)
Fritz Domenowski	*Maschinenobermaat*	Electric Motor Mate
Werner Rieckhoff	*Maschinenobergefreiter*	Control Room Stoker (*U 2521)
Johann Rebahn	*Maschinenobergefreiter*	Control Room Stoker (*U 674)
Hans Merk	*Maschinenobergefreiter*	Control Room Stoker
Reinhold Abel	*Maschinenobergefreiter*	Starboard Diesel Stoker
Walter Labahn	*Maschinenobergefreiter*	Port Diesel Stoker
Werner Schlägel	*Maschinenobergefreiter*	Starboard Diesel Stoker (*U 540)
Helmut Brock	*Maschinengefreiter*	Port Diesel Stoker
Walter Heinrich	*Maschinenobergefreiter*	E-Motor Stoker
Ludwig Sass	*Maschinenobergefreiter*	E Motor Stoker
Phillip Wärner	*Maschinenobergefreiter*	E-Motor Stoker (*U 678)

When U 564 went to the bottom of the Bay of Biscay on 14 June 1943, she carried the bodies of twenty-eight crewmen with her (* indicates present on board during U 564's patrol between July and September 1942):

Ernst Möller	*Oberleutnant (Ing.)*
Erich Zapf	*Obermaschinist*
Walter Christ	*Obermaschinist*
Wilhelm Steinhauer	*Obermaschinenmaat*
Fritz Hummel	*Obermaschinenmaat**
Joseph Harsch	*Obermaschinenmaat**
Alfred Meidorn	*Maschinenmaat*
Otfried Lehmann	*Maschinenmaat*
Kurt Rothbarth	*Maschinenmaat*
Fritz Hild	*Mechanikermaat*
Erich Stuttner	*Mechanikerobergefreiter*
Paul Stephan	*Matrosenobergefreiter**
Richard Steinert	*Matrosenobergefreiter**
Joseph Pledl	*Maschinenobergefreiter*
Paul Tolksdorf	*Maschinengefreiter*
Karl Meyer	*Maschinengefreiter*

Werner Heinze	Maschinengefreiter
Karl Fischer	Maschinengefreiter
Walter Grassl	Maschinengefreiter
Max Hartleb	Maschinengefreiter
Günther Schwaiger	Maschinengefreiter
Heinz Mistereck	Maschinengefreiter
Fritz Pfanz	Maschinengefreiter
Hermann Mähler	Maschinengefreiter
Rudi Elkerhausen	Oberfunkmaat*
Werner Weise	Funkmaat
Werner Apitz	Funkobergefreiter*
Peter Geise	Funker

APPENDIX TWO: TORPEDOES FIRED BY *U564*

Between 1 July and 30 September 1942

Date	Grid	Torp.	Target	Est. grt	Actual target	grt	Result
19/7	CE3341	G7e	Steamer	5,000	*Empire Hawksbill*	5,724	Hit, sunk.
19/7	CE3341	G7e	Steamer	5,000	*Lavington Court*	5,372	Hit, sunk
19/7	CE3341	G7e	Liner	8,000	—	—	Claimed sunk
19/7	CD3341	G7e	Steamer	5,000	—	—	Claimed sunk
19/8	ED9460	G7e	Steamer	—	—	—	Missed
19/8	ED9460	G7e	Steamer	—	—	—	Missed
19/8	ED9460	G7e	Steamer	—	—	—	Missed
19/8	ED9460	G7e	Steamer	—	—	—	Missed
19/8	ED9460	G7e	Steamer	—	—	—	Missed
19/8	ED9453	G7e	Steamer	8,000	*British Consul*	6,940	Hit , sunk
19/8	ED9453	G7a	Steamer	7,000	*Empire Cloud*	5,969	Hit, sunk
19/8	ED9453	G7e	Steamer	8,000	—	—	Claimed damaged
19/8	ED9453	G7e	Steamer	5,000	—	—	Claimed damaged
19/8	ED9416	G7e	Steamer	—	—	—	Hit, un-exploded
19/8	ED9416	G7e	Steamer	—	—	—	Hit, un-exploded
30/8	EE9933	G7a	Tanker	9,000	*Vardaas*	8,176	Hit, dam-aged
30/8	EE9933	G7a	Tanker	9,000	*Vardaas*	8,176	Missed
Sinking by gunfire							
30/8	EE9933	—	Tanker	9,000	*Vardaas*	8,176	35 hits, sunk

Sources, Bibliography, Suggested Reading

Wiedersehen in Hamburg-A Souvenir of the Meeting of U-Boat Men, May 1954, Bücherdienst Herbert Zeissler, Hamburg-Wandsbek, 1954.

British Admiralty Anti-U-Boat Warfare Reports, 1942. Held at the Royal Navy Submarine Museum).

Public Records Office, File ADM237/145. Relates to Convoy OS.34.

Kriegstagebuch (KTB) *U 564*. Photocopy held at U-Boot Archiv.

KTB 1st U-Flotilla. NARA microfilm, T1022, Roll 3403.

KTB BdU, July to September 1942. NARA microfilm, T1022, Rolls 3980, 3981.

Wet Oakleaves. An excellent unofficial translation of *Nasses Eichenlaub*, by courtesy of Frank James.

Published Books

Blair, Clay, *Hitler's U-Boat War*, Vols 1 & 2, Cassell, 1996.

Bowyer, Chaz, *Men Of Coastal Command 1939–1945*, William Kimber, 1985.

Dönitz, Karl, *Ten Years And Twenty Days*, Lionel Leventhal, 1990.

Franks, Norman, *Conflict Over The Bay*, William Kimber, 1986.

———, *Search, Find And Kill*, Grub Street, 1995.

Gabler, Ulrich, *Submarine Design*, Bernard & Graefe, 1986.

Herzog, Bodo, *Deutsche U-Boote 1906 – 1966*, Karl Müller Verlag, 1996.

Hessler, Günter, *The U-Boat War in the Atlantic*, HMSO, 1989.

Hildebrand, Hans, and Lohmann, Werner, *Die Deutsche Kriegsmarine 1939–1945*, Podzun-Verlag, 1956.

Kelshall, *The U-Boat War in the Caribbean*, United States Naval Institute, 1994.

Martienssen, Anthony, *Führer Conferences on Naval Affairs*, HMSO, 1948.

Mulligan, Timothy, *Neither Sharks Nor Wolves*, Naval Institute Press, 1999.

Niestlé, Axel, *German U-Boat Losses During World War Two*, Naval Institute Press, 1998.

Paterson, Lawrence, *First U-Boat Flotilla*, Pen & Sword, 2001.

———, *Second U-Boat Flotilla*, Pen & Sword, 2003.

Price, Alfred, *Aircraft Versus Submarine*, Naval Institute Press, 1974.

Rohwer, Jürgen, *Axis Submarine Successes*, Naval Institute Press, 1983.

Rössler, Eberhard, *The U-Boat War*, Arms & Armour Press, 1981.

Rust, Eric C., *Naval Officers Under Hitler*, Praeger, 1991.

Showell, Jak P. Mallmann, *U-Boat Command and the Battle of the Atlantic*, Conway Maritime Press, 1989.

Stern, Robert C., *Type VII U-Boat*, Arms & Armour, 1991.

Suhren, Reinhard, and Fritz, Brustat, *Nasses Eichenlaub*, Koehlers Verlag, 1983.

Topp, Erich, *Fackeln über dem Atlantik*, E. S. Mittler & Sohn, 1990.

U-Boat Commander's Handbook, The. Thomas Publications, 1943). Translation.

Wynn, Kenneth, *U-Boat Operations of the Second World War*, Vols 1 & 2, Chatham Publishing, 1997.

Suggested Websites

U-boat.net (http://www.uboat.net)

The U-Boat War (http://www.uboatwar.net)

Grey Wolf (http://www.u-boot-greywolf.de)

Norwegian Merchant Fleet 1939–1945 (http://www.warsailors.com)

U-Boat Archive: Photographs and Records of the U-Boat War (http://www.uboatarchive.net/)

Deutsche U-Boote 1935–1945 (http://www.u-boot-archiv.de)

SubArt (http://www.subart.net)

Notes

Introduction

1. Interview with Hans Rudolf Rösing, 12 October 2001.
2. Established on 7 October 1736 by August III, King of Poland and Elector of Saxony, it was second only to Saxony's Order of the Crown of Rue; the Military Order of St Henry was awarded to serving officers, either for conspicuous personal bravery on the battlefield or, more frequently in the case of officers of higher rank, for merit in positions of great responsibility.
3. Interview with Hans Rudolf Rösing, October 2001.
4. *Dresdner Anzelger*, 11 November 1940; quotation from *Frau* Ernestine Suhren, Teddy's mother.
5. Suhren, Reinhard, *Nasses Eichenlaub*, p. 13.
6. *Ibid.*, p. 15.
7. *Ibid.*, p. 16.
8. The previous year, the commander of the *Emden* had been *Fregattenkapitän* Karl Dönitz, a man soon to play a major role in Suhren's life.
9. *Nasses Eichenlaub*, p. 19.
10. Ibid., p. 32.
11. Interestingly, his brother Gerd had also become the first Engineering Officer to be awarded the Knight's Cross, on 21 October 1940.
12. Interview with Hans Rudolf Rösing, 12 October 2001.
13. Nasses Eichenlaub, pp. 68–9.
14. Excerpt from Suhren's speech, Hamburg, 1954, published in *Wiedersehen in Hamburg*, 1954.
15. By July 1942, *U 564* had sunk thirteen ships, totalling 63,346grt, and seriously damaged five others.
16. *Nasses Eichenlaub*, p. 113.
17. Busch, Harald, *So War der U-Boot Krieg*.

Chapter One

1. During the months of May and June, *U 564* operated off the coast of Florida, sinking four ships and damaging three others.
2. Geisler had served aboard *U 564* since its commissioning. Son and namesake of a Knight's Cross-holding *Luftwaffe* General, Geisler subsequently held various training and administrative posts, ending the war as commander of the Type XXI *U 3049*, although this boat was still under construction at the end of hostilities.
3. Interview with Reinhard Suhren, 1981, A1981/22/002, Royal Navy Submarine Museum.
4. By the end of the year, 'Triton' had finally been broken, and from then until the end of the war only periodic brief lapses were suffered by the Allies in reading German coded messages.
5. Interview with Reinhard Suhren, 1981, A1981/22/002, Royal Navy Submarine Museum.

6. *U 564* KTB.
7. *U 751* was not the first Biscay casualty for July 1942. Jürgen von Rosenstiel's *U 502* had been depth-charged by a No 172 Squadron Wellington bomber on 6 July — the first successful sinking using the newly introduced Leigh Light.

Chapter 2

1. *U 564* KTB.
2. See Paterson, *First U-Boat Flotilla*, pp. 138–40.
3. Dönitz had earmarked the château for his personal use before Hitler ordered him to Paris following the Allied raid on St-Nazaire. Thus, Rösing and his fortunate staff inherited the building — which was fully equipped. The chart copy was maintained as a back-up in the event of damage to the main chart at BdU headquarters.
4. HMS *Erne* had been scheduled to sail with OS.33 but had been withheld after being deemed by the Admiralty to have had 'insufficient practices and cannot be considered efficient'. Thus *Erne* remained in Britain for flotilla exercises before joining the 15th Escort Group.
5. HMS *Gorleston* had begun life as the US Coast Guard Cutter *Itasca*. She was transferred to the Royal Navy in 1941 under the Lend-Lease agreement.
6. *U 564* KTB.
7. After Action Analysis, Lt-Cdr Gibson, Senior Officer 42nd Escort Group, PRO ADM 237/145.
8. *Nasses Eichenlaub*, p. 104.
9. *Ibid.*, p. 106.
10. *U 564* KTB.
11. The prefix 'Empire' was given to ships that the British Ministry of Shipping ordered built for the British Government or to those purchased, taken as war prizes or requisitioned. The Ministry of Shipping merged with the Ministry of Transport to become the Ministry of War Transport (MOWT) in 1941. A total of 196 vessels of the 'Empire' range were sunk during the Second World War.
12. *Nasses Eichenlaub*, p. 108.
13. Two other canisters were developed for launching from the *Pillenwerfer*. The first was a miniature torpedo that carried no warhead but an electric motor that would circle at a given depth and simulate the noise created by a U-boat's electric drive before its small battery became exhausted. The second more closely mirrored Hitler's original intention and contained oil which rose to the surface, creating a small slick for attackers to see. Neither saw operational use.
14. Suhren may well have benefited from a freak accident during *Gorleston*'s Operation 'Raspberry'. Blast from one of the depth charges had hurled debris and petrol from the disintegrated *Empire Hawksbill* through the sloop's open wheelhouse window, temporarily blinding all exposed personnel.
15. Interview with Herbert Waldschmidt, 27 September 2002.
16. *Nasses Eichenlaub*, p. 110.
17. PRO ADM 237/145.
18. Report on Proceedings from HMS *Gorleston*'s captain, PRO, ADM 237/145.
19. *Nasses Eichenlaub*, p. 111.
20. *Ibid.*, p. 112.
21. *Ibid.*, p. 115.

Chapter 3

1. Interview with Georg Seitz, Mannheim 2000.

2. *Nasses Eichenlaub*, . p112.
3. *Ibid.*, p. 76.
4. Interview with Reinhard Suhren, 1981, A1981/22/002, Royal Navy Submarine Museum.

Chapter 4
1. *U 564* KTB.
2. The 10th U-Flotilla's headquarters were situated in Lorient. Shortly afterwards, *U 463* and all the other tankers were transferred to the newly raised 12th U-Flotilla, centred at Bordeaux. After four successful refuelling voyages, *U 463* was attacked and sunk on 16 May 1943 by an RAF Halifax bomber from No 58 Squadron south-west of the Scilly Isles and lost with all fifty-three men aboard. By June 1944, following a concerted Allied drive to 'kill' the tankers, all ten operational *Milchkühe* had been destroyed.
3. Interview with Herbert Waldschmidt, 27 September 2002.
4. After 60 hours in their lifeboats, the Norwegian steamer *Nordstjernan* rescued the Swedish vessel's crew.

Chapter 5
1. Interview with Reinhard Suhren, 1981 (A1981/22/002), Royal Navy Submarine Museum.
2. See Paterson, *Second U-Boat Flotilla*, p. 136.
3. They were later landed at Guantanamo Bay, Cuba.
4. The fifty-one men were later landed variously at Key West, Florida, and Mobile, Alabama.

Chapter 6
1. Interview with Reinhard Suhren, 1981, A1981/22/002, Royal Navy Submarine Museum.
2. Wattenberg and his men were later handed over to American intelligence officers, who found them disciplined and security-conscious. Wattenburg, the former communications officer aboard *Admiral Graf Spee*, was later housed in an Arizona POW camp in Papago Park, from where he hatched and mounted an ambitious escape plan. Along with twenty-four others, he escaped via a 250-foot tunnel, picked through solid granite with screwdrivers and coal shovels. Of those who attained freedom, Wattenburg was at liberty the longest — thirty-six days — before being recaptured in Phoenix.
3. *Nasses Eichenlaub*, p. 123.

Epilogue
1. Gabler formed the Ingenieurkontor Lübeck company in 1946, specialising in submarine design. He retired in January 1979.
2. *U 564* KTB.
3. Excerpt from Suhren's speech, Hamburg, May 1954, published in *Wiedersehen in Hamburg*, 1954.
4. Author interview, 19 October 2002, Munich.
5. US Navy, Interrogation report of Klaus Bargsten, O.N.I. 250–G/serial 14.
6. 1st U-Flotilla KTB, 14 July 1943.
7. After three nights in a rubber dinghy, Benson and his four crewmen were rescued by the French fishingtrawler *Jazz Band*. They were subsequently landed at Morgat on the Crozon peninsula and handed over to German troops stationed there.

8. Rösing and Suhren were held primarily to be called as witnesses in the Nuremburg trial of Karl Dönitz. They were determined to speak in their *Grossadmiral*'s defence, but they were never called.
9. Erich Topp, *Odyssey of a U-Boat Commander*, pp. 82–4.

≡ Index

Entries in italics are ship names; page numbers in italics refer to photographs